GUITAR CHOR HEAVEN

Guitar Chord Heaven
Compiled by Roger Manning

Concept created by Clive Gregory

Edited by: Clive Gregory

Chord progressions composed by Roger Manning & Clive Gregory

Music specially composed by Clive Gregory & Roger Manning

Photographs by: R & C Gregory Publishing Limited

Artwork and design: R & C Gregory Publishing Limited

Text and music typeset by R & C Gregory Publishing Limited

Imposition by Spectrum Graphics, Bexleyheath.

Special thanks to: Rubiah Gregory, Peter Wall, Roger Manning and Clive Sayer without whom this book would not have been possible.

We've lost count of the number of people that have suggested this book be made - all of whom have offered their advice help and support:
Clive Sayer & Roger Manning - Beat 'n' Track, Tonbridge. Danny 'maj 9' Prendergast - Aylesbury Music (Oktober).
Graham Mitchell & Eric Snow - American Guitar Centre, Maidstone. Richard Cholerton - Regent Guitars, Leamington.
Howard & Terry - Oasis Music, Ringwood. Shea Rider & Carl - Rockbottom, Croydon.
Steve Treble - Treblerock Music, Bristol. Mike & gang - Bonners, Eastbourne. Peter Lancaster - Impact Music, Brighton.
Tony Bird - Birds Music, Bexhill. Mark Griffin - Stag Music, Trowbridge. Pete & Cath - TMT, Orpington.
Paul & Mark Cleaver - DB Music, Bristol. Graham Plummer & gang - Music Exchange, Manchester.
John Hillary - Madcap, Westbury. Mac - Mac's Music, Herne Bay. Richard & gang - Socodi Music, Canterbury.
Roy - The Music Place, Letchworth. Andy Bole, Bole Music, Sutton Coldfield. John Williams & John Settle - Noise Works,
Coventry. Tim Kelsall & gang - TMC, Coventry. Richard & gang - Kingfisher Music, Fleet. Eric Lindsay - EL Music, Catford &
Reigate. Paul Hart - Monster Music, Worthing. John & Steve - John Boots Music, Hythe. Dick & Richard - Patrick-Reed Music,
Kettering. Bruce & Simon - Music Centre, Bedford. Mark - MusicLand , Chatham. Glen - Wavelength, Sheffield.
Ian - Planet Guitars, Wycombe. Matt & Lou - Supreme Drums, London. Rupert - Soundgarden, Barnet.
Pete = Theme Music, Hendon. Paul Holmes - Holmes Music, Swindon. Roger - Jailhouse, Tenterden.

First edition, published 2002

Published by
R & C Gregory Publishing Limited

Suite 7, Unit 6, Beckenham Business Centre, Cricket Lane, Kent. BR3 1LB

ISBN 1 901690 69 5

Printed by COLOURSCOPE OFFSET LIMITED, Beckenham, England.

INTRODUCTION the purpose of this book.

CONTENTS

Congratulations on buying Guitar Chord Heaven. This really is the ultimate guitar chord reference for ALL guitarists because for the first time there is a chord dictionary that explains how chords are used. Guitar Chord Heaven is also a library of chord progressions to aid your knowledge and help you with your writing and ideas.

Guitar Chord Heaven is a thorough chord dictionary illustrated with standard guitar chord boxes, supported by hundreds of photographs, tab and music notation. Each chord type has been set to a practical chord progression so that you can immediately try out a chord in the context of a real chord progression.

There is no standard as such, either in the level of difficulty with individual chords or chord progressions or CD tracks. Some are easy, some tricky.

Each method of illustration is fully explained on the next page. The dictionary is laid out alphabetically which makes it simple and unambiguous to find any chord you are trying to find and learn.

You actually need no musical knowledge or guitar skills to find chords in this book. This book will show you how to play 312 different chords - with all the variations that's 1680 chord shapes for you to choose from. There are 672 chords that we've given priority status and each of these chords is accompanied by a photograph, music notation, tab and, of course, a standard guitar box or fret box.

What makes this book extra special are the chord progressions. It is always helpful to know which chords could precede or follow a chord you've referenced. Every main chord type (there are 20 main groups in this book) in every key has a 4 bar chord progression specially created for it. That means there are 240 chord progressions to choose from. Add 30 progressions written for the CD and you have 270 progressions. Each one can help you learn, play and create music.

Chord progressions in their basic form are in the public domain, i.e. "G - C - Am" is not copyright. If you we're to create an arrangement or composition based on these chords, that had a specific rhythm and voicing (the precise arrangement of notes in a chord), then this arrangement would belong to you. So all progressions, although specially compiled and devised for this book, are generic progressions and free for anybody to use.

The integral CD has 21 music tracks, each one specially written and produced to accompany this book. Each track is designed to show off one chord type in particular, i.e "major", "minor 7" "13" etc.. The compositions are detailed on pages 54-55. Tracks 1-20 of the CD demonstrate every 'photo-chord' with an E root, see page 54 for details. You can easily practise soloing to the CD tracks, which are easy to play-along with for either rhythm or lead.

The following few pages will show you how chords are created and how they relate to one another. This is true Guitar Chord Heaven because one chord in isolation is like having one piece of a jigsaw. The book is not a tutor book as such but the following sections will give you enough information to understand basic chord construction, the way a chord relates to the scale and key and from there, how one chord relates to another.

We'll also describe the common chord progressions. If you're new to chords and music you'll be astounded by the number of songs that use the same chord progressions. This is not always so easy to tell at first, especially if you have little or no understanding about how keys work. Don't worry, this book will show you how to spot the same chord progressions from song to song.

It will become apparent how it is possible for musicians to be able to play along to a song (sometimes called 'busk' a song) when they've never played or heard the song before. If you know that many songs use the same chord progression you can learn to recognise these progressions when you hear them. You can also anticipate the most likely next chord through this knowledge.

Of course there is plenty of music that is complex and composers and arrangers like to write music that sounds fresh and new. Chords and chord progressions can be disguised by skilful writing but in a lot of music the basics of a common chord progression still exist in much music that sounds really complicated. Much of this is beyond the scope of this book but we will try to sow the seeds of how chords are put together and the ways they can be added to and modified.

So , you can use this book to look up the odd chord when you're stuck and you can also use this book to become a chord expert by studying chord construction and by learning and studying the chord progressions.

If you need more help studying , then "Learn Guitar - from beginner to your first band" is available now!

GUIDE TO USING THIS BOOK

Please take a moment to read this section so that you understand each element in the book and how to make best use of it.

The elements:

1.   Chord symbol and information box
2.   Photograph
3.   Chord box
4.   Tab
5.   Music notation
6.   Chord progression
7.   CD tracks

1. The Chord Symbol and information box

Chord symbols are usually all you get in songbooks or written down by other musicians. Always read the information box as it will tell you the correct symbol, name and sometimes alternative name for the chord. The notes that make up a chord are also detailed here, as is a brief description of the chord and how it's constructed.

2. The Chord Box (fret box)

There are two sizes of chord box. The larger box accompanies a photo and is used for all the essential chords. The smaller boxes are used for the 'bonus' chords - that might be useful used. In both cases where to place each additional chord shapes but are less commonly the box shows precisely finger on the fingerboard. There is a number in each finger dot, so that you're in no doubt which finger goes where.

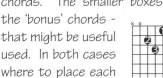

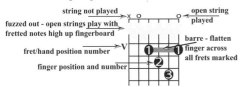

3. The Photograph

There is a photograph for all of the most essential chords. The photo shows how your hand should look when playing the chord. This should be used as an aid to technique as well as a visual aid for where to put each finger. Don't worry if you can't play a chord as comfortably as it looks in the photo - practise makes perfect. However, always use the photo in conjunction with the chord box: As in the example above , there is usually some compromise, such as tucking an unused finger out of the way to enable the photo to show which notes are being played. Just let unused fingers relax in their most natural position, don't copy this aspect of the photo.

4. Tab notation

Tab will be familiar to most guitarists and is an optional method of viewing the chord and how to play it. It is simple to understand: Each line represents a string, the lowest line = the lowest string. A number is

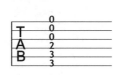

placed on or over each line/string that is to be played. This number represents the FRET number to be played. The example to the left therefore means - play the 3rd fret on both the (low) E string and the A string, play the 2nd fret on the D string and play open strings on the G, B and (high) E strings.

5. Music notation.

Music notation is used for the benefit of reading musicians and for those that would like to read music or improve their reading. "Learn Guitar - from beginner to your first band", will teach you how to read music

well. In brief it works like this: The five lines do not represent guitar strings in any way. These make up the 'staff'. Onto this staff you place a clef, which positions notes on the staff. Notes can be placed on the lines or in the spaces. A quick way to understand which note is which, is learn the notes on the lines, from the lowest to the highest are: E - G - B - D - F. The spaces are (from the first full space above the line): F - A - C - E - G.

6. Chord Progressions

Every chord type is put into context with its own chord progression for you to try out. The level of technical difficulty varies. The brief descriptions that accompany each progression will further enhance your knowledge of a given chord and how and where to use it. The exact chord shapes to use are for you to experiment with. Some examples recommend that you keep a particular note as your highest note throughout, or that you ensure a melody is created by the chords.

7. CD tracks

CD TRACKS - see pages 54-55. Each chord type; "major", "minor", "major 7" etc. has a CD track designed to show it off. Obviously each composition contains several chords, so across all tracks you should get to know each chord quite well. Most CD tracks are composed around a 'classic' chord progression, that is a chord progression that's been used on thousands of songs.

CHORD CONSTRUCTION - How to make a chord!

A chord is defined as three or more notes heard (played) at the same time. The magical thing about chords is that although they are made up of a number of individual notes we don't really hear these individual notes we hear a rich blend of sounds. In fact it takes quite a bit of practise to 'hear' the individual notes that make up chords.

The simplest chord is known as a triad, a triad is a chord made up of three notes. However, the three notes are not just random notes they are drawn from specific notes of the scale.

So, let's start by understanding a scale first. All music around the globe begins with a scale. A scale is just a collection of different frequencies or pitches (notes) that are organised from the lowest note to the highest note. There are an infinite number of pitches and so, in theory, an infinite number of scales. Fortunately, most western music uses scales made up of only 7 different notes. Once you have a collection of 7 different named notes, you can describe this set of notes as a 'scale', collectively called the 'key'.

As you have probably already discovered, your guitar has 12 frets between the open string note and the 12th fret, where the same note name is repeated. You don't usually find all these 'chromatic' notes being used to make up a melody - as mentioned above, our common scale uses only 7 notes. However, each of these 12 notes CAN be the start of a new key, or set of 7 notes.

This book describes 26 different types of chords (in 20 groups) for each of the 12 keys - beginning with the key of A.

To summarise, there are 12 different keys - each containing 7 different notes. A different letter of the alphabet is used to describe these 7 notes, which is why the musical alphabet contains only the letters; A-B-C-D-E-F-G. To enable us to keep this simple idea, and still deal with 12 different keys, each note can become either sharp (#) or flat (♭) - (strictly we call "A", A natural). The sharp version of a note is a fret (semi-tone) higher than the natural note and the flat version is a fret (semi-tone) lower than the natural note. (Higher on a guitar means moving your finger towards you and flat away from you.)

You may find it confusing at first trying to deal with the idea that, for example, "G#" is the same note (and key) as A♭. Most of the time it doesn't matter which name you call it - so don't worry about it.

As well as the note names (A, B, C etc.) musicians also identify notes by the order of the notes in the scale, numbered accordingly 1 -7 (Roman numerals are used when writing; I-II-III-IV-V-VI-VII). You'll understand how useful this can be in the next couple of pages.

Back to the triad!

The specific notes of the scale that the common triad uses are the first note, the third note and the fifth note. The first note of a chord is always called the ROOT note and the other notes of the chord are called by their position in the scale, THIRD and FIFTH. You'll hear the terms ROOT, THIRD and FIFTH all the time when chord construction is being discussed. To help clarify exactly which notes I mean I'll put some note names on this. The key of C major uses the following notes: C, D, E, F, G, A and B (all natural notes). To build a triad, take the first, third and fifth notes of this scale; C - E and G. Play these notes together

as a chord and you have a chord of C major, yes it really is that simple.

In addition, you have two main key types. Major and minor. Confusingly at first, the two types share a set of notes. If you begin with the notes of a major scale, go up to the sixth note and rearrange the notes, starting on this sixth note, you get the minor scale. So for C major, count up six (= "A") and create the new scale; A, B, C, D, E, F, G. this 'new' scale is the scale (key) of "A" minor. The difference in character from the bright, positive major sound to the more laid back and melancholic minor, is brought about by the different intervals between each note. (Scales are made up of tones (2 fret intervals) and semi-tones (1 fret intervals).

The character of the scale types as mentioned above, is similar for the 2 chord types of major and minor. The good news is although there are 26 different chord types in this book, they are nearly all variations of either major or minor chords. This means that you create many chords by adding different notes to either the major or minor triads. Mostly this is done, as with the triad, by taking each odd numbered note, so; 1st, 3rd, 5th (=triad) then 7th, 9th, 11th and 13th. The last note added gives the chord its name, so if you add a 7th to the triad it'll be called a "7" chord, if you add 7th and 9th, it's a "9" chord and so on. Chords named in this way assume that you add on notes, so a "13" chord 'should' contain; Root, 3rd, 5th, 7th, 9th, 11th and 13th (yes all the notes from the scale). In practice, most chords are 'cut down' in some way, let's face it, you can't play a 7 note chord with only 6 strings. What is important is the character of each chord. A professional guitarist can capture the character of even a "13" chord with 4 or 5 notes. These pro' chords are sometimes called partial chords and usually they work fine on their own, sometimes they come about from working with other musicians (for example, why play the root of a chord if the bass player is playing it). It is important to learn these shapes as well and to think of these shapes as being the full chord. We have tried to give you a mixture of 'text book correct' chords and 'pro' chords in this book.

Other chords can be constructed by altering certain notes. An augmented chord is created by taking a major triad and raising the 5th by one fret. You could also alter an added note so "A7#9" is a chord of "A" with the 7th and 9th added to the triad ("A9") but the 9th has been altered - sharpened by 1 fret in this case. Sometimes a chord is created by adding one specific note to the triad, so "C6", for example adds the 6th note to the major triad. Other chords created in this way need to stipulate that they are being added to the triad by using the word... "add" - amazing. E.g. "C add9".

NOTE: Some chords have small labels within a chord type section, these are as follows:

"major9" is chord No. 10 in "major 7" section.
"9" and "add9' chords are both in the "9" chord section.
"m9 and "m add9" are both in the "m9" chord section.
"m11" is chord No. 5 in "minor 13" chord section.
"11" is chord No. 5 in "13" chord section
There are 3 types of diminished chord: the diminished triad (labelled "°"), (root, ♭3rd, ♭5th), "m7♭5" (root, ♭3rd, ♭5th & 7th) and "°7" (root, ♭3rd, ♭5th & ♭♭7th) all three variations are found in the diminished group section.

CHORD PROGRESSIONS - One chord into another!

Playing one chord at a time is a fairly meaningless exercise. Songs are made up of a number of chords each played for a set number of beats and then moving off into another chord. This is a chord progression.

OK, if you're playing a Beatles song or an Oasis song and you've got the chord progression written down in front of you, you've got this dictionary and away you go - a bit of practise and you're playing the Beatles.

If, on the other hand you've got a tune in your head, a guitar in your hand and you want to write a song, then you may find it's not quite so easy.

So just how do you figure out which chord to play next or how do you find that special chord to make your writing more sophisticated.

We'll it's back to our friends the scale and the key to begin to understand how it all works. Look again at the key of C major, here are all the notes in this key; C - D - E - F - G - A - B. You've seen how to create a chord of C major from these few notes. However, the chord of C major is only one possible chord. If you can get a chord by starting on the letter C, then you can get another chord by starting on the letter D. If you begin on "D" (the root) then the third will be "F" (d, e, f) and the fifth is "A". So you have a chord containing D - F - A. This is the chord of "D minor".

OK, you've spotted the problem, how do you know it's a minor chord; "D minor". Well, you could buy "Learn Guitar - from beginner to your 1st Band" and learn more about keys, or the quick way is to learn which type of chord is created on each note of the scale, as follows:

> 1st note (I) = MAJOR
> 2nd note (II) = MINOR
> 3rd note (III) = MINOR
> 4th note (IV) = MAJOR
> 5th note (V) = MAJOR
> 6th note (VI)= MINOR
> 7th note (VII)= DIMINISHED.

This, when translated into the key of C major gives you the following 7 chords;

> (I) = C MAJOR
> (II) = D MINOR
> (III) = E MINOR
> (IV) = F MAJOR
> (V) = G MAJOR
> (VI)= A MINOR
> (VII)= B DIMINISHED.

From the above chords we can make up the vast stock of the common (or 'classic') chord progressions because most common chord progressions use chords from the same key. It is perfectly possible to have chord progressions that change key as the music progresses but I'll concentrate on staying in the same key for now.

To illustrate what is meant by a common chord progression we'll start with the commonest of the lot. Look at the chord types built on each note of the scale (major or minor) and you'll see that on the first, fourth and fifth notes of the scale you have the same chord type. Before I go any further get used to the idea that from now on I'm going to describe chords according to their position within the scale, i.e. the chord built on the first note of the scale is known as the **I** (ONE) chord and the chord built on the fourth note of the scale is the **IV** (FOUR) chord etc..

[Remember the convention when writing this down is to use roman numerals. I, II, III, IV, V, VI & VII .]

To make it easy to hear what I'm talking about learn 3 easy chords. "G", "C" and "D" major or minor (or both). If you don't know these already then learn them now before reading on.

In the "G" scale the **I, IV** and **V** are, respectively, "G", "C" and "D". These are the chords that make up what's known as the **'three chord trick'**. Play the chords one after the other, then mix them about a bit - instant music - instant song, well almost. However you arrange them, you're bound to create something recognisable. Thousands of hit songs have used no more than three chords. Possibly the commonest way of arranging the **I, IV** and **V** is in a 12 bar blues format. See CD track 23, detailed on page 54. Play along using the regular "G", "C" and "D" chords you've just learned (assuming you're a beginner) or if you already know them use the "7" chords. A number of our CD tracks use the three chord trick in some way.

Classic chord progressions are progressions that are used time and time again by songwriters and composers, there's no getting away from them. Sure, it's nice to compose something a little different but make sure you know this lot - they'll recur throughout this book's chord progressions along with many more - ENJOY:

Major	Minor
II - V - I	I - VII - VI - V7
I - VI - II - V	I - IV - VII - III - VI - II° - V7
I - VI - IV - V	I - III - VI - V7
I - VI - IV - III7	II - V - I
III - VI - IV - V into I - IV - V	I - V - VI - VII
I - IV - VI - V	IV - VII - V - I

5

A — A - C♯ - E

A Major

The major triad is built using the 1st, 3rd and 5th notes from the major scale. It's the building block for all major & dominant chords.

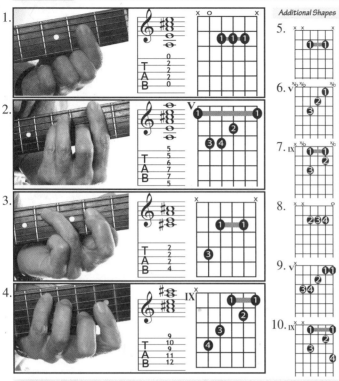

Additional Shapes

Classic chord progression with A in the strong 1 position - note how E7 gives strength to the A chord on repeat.

I	VI	IV	V
A	F♯m7	D	E7

A△7(9) — A - C♯ - E - G♯ - (B)

A Major 7
(A Major 9)

Add the 7th note from the major scale to the major triad. The classic 'chill out' chord, very relaxed. Add 9th note for 'more'.

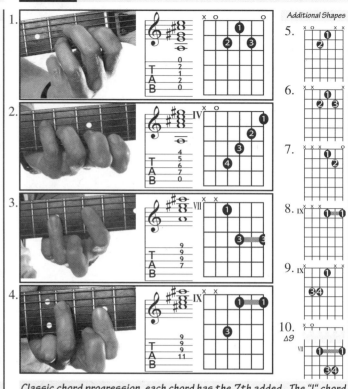

Additional Shapes

Classic chord progression, each chord has the 7th added. The "I" chord wil always be major 7, as will "IV", only the "V" chord is dominant 7.

I	VI	II	V
A△7	F♯m7	Bm7	E7

A7 — A - C♯ - E - G

A dominant 7

Add the 7th note from the minor scale to the MAJOR triad. Found mainly on the 5th note of the scale - powering back to the "I" chord.

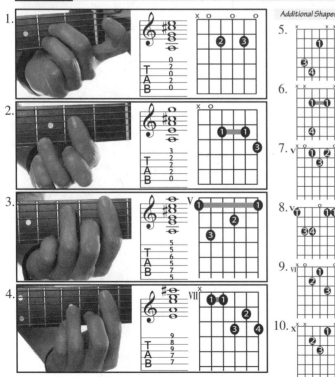

Additional Shapes

Common progression. All chords are dominant 7 ("7") chords, therefore the key changes each chord - typical of most 'bluesy' music.

I	IV	V	V
A7	D7	E	E7

A9 — A - C♯ - E - (G) - B

A9 and A add9 (A2)

The shapes of '9' and 'add 9' are similar but the sound of the full 9 chord is jazzier than 'add 9', as it includes the 7th.

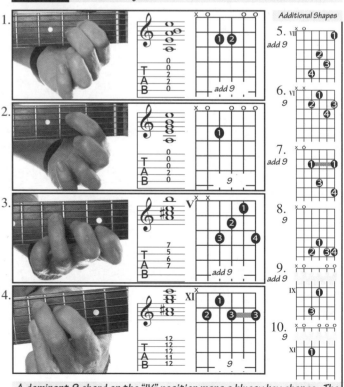

Additional Shapes

A dominant 9 chord on the "IV" position mans a bluesy key change. The "B" in the chord holds things together and remains the link throughout.

I	IV	III	VI₇
E	A9	G♯m7	C♯9

Am A - C - E

A Minor — The minor triad is built using the 1st, 3rd and 5th notes from the minor scale. It's the building block for all minor chords.

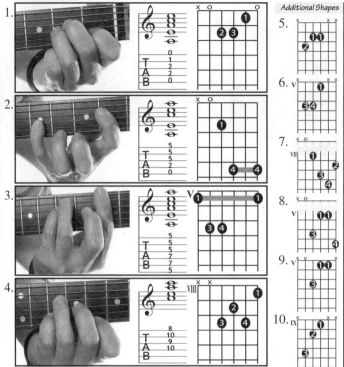

Additional Shapes

Well worn progression that remains in the same key with Am as the fairly weak sounding "III" chord.

I	V	III	VI7	V
F	C	Am	Dm7	C

Am7 A - C - E - G

A Minor 7 — Add the 7th note from the minor scale to the minor triad. The character is milder, not so melancholic as the minor triad but is less positive.

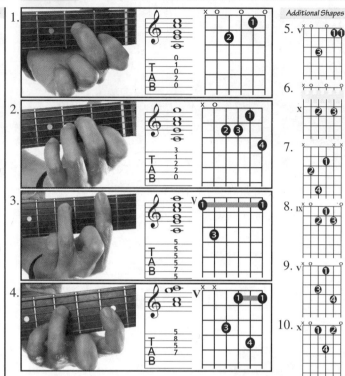

Additional Shapes

Am7 in the "III" position. Although weak sounding when following a "V" chord, after "I" "IV" it's much bolder, the 7th adds to this effect.

I	IV	III	VI	II	V
F△7	Bb△7	Am7	Dm7	Gm9	C11

Am9 A - C - E - (G) - B

Am9 and Am add9 — The shapes of 'm9' and 'm add 9' are similar but the sound of the 'm add9' chord is more 'mystic' than 'm9', as it omits the 7th.

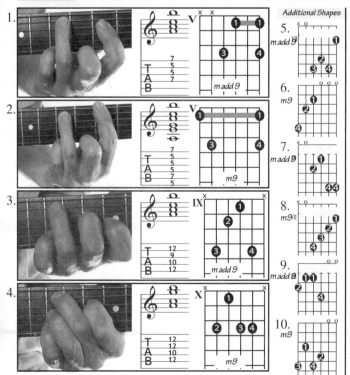

Additional Shapes

Classic chord progression is disguised and smoothed by extending chords (adding 7 and 9). The Am9 retains "E", "G" and "B" from Em chord.

VI	II	V	I
Em7	Am9	D11	G△7

A° diminished group A - C - Eb - (G(b))

A°, A°7 & Am7b5 — Diminished chords have similar fingerings and uses, the m7b5 adds a minor 7th and for °7 flatten the minor 7th another fret.

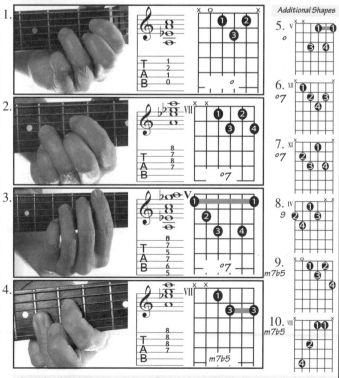

Additional Shapes

Standard minor progression. This is very common in jazz and latin ballads and standards - remains firmly in G minor.

I	I	II	V	V7
Gm	Gm	Am7b5	D/A	D7

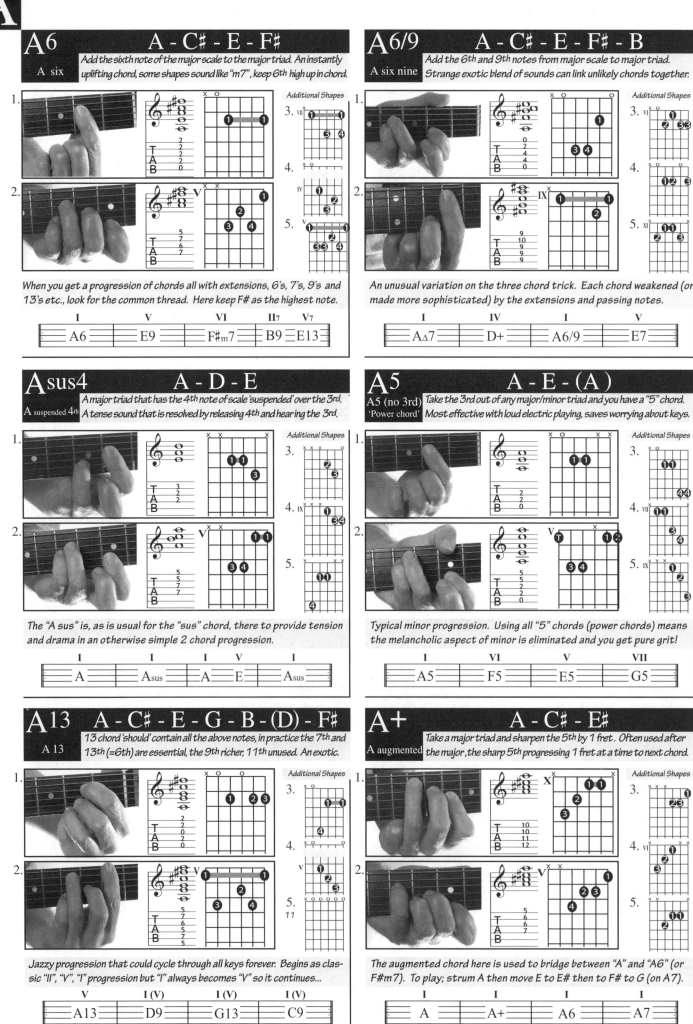

A6   A - C♯ - E - F♯

A six

Add the sixth note of the major scale to the major triad. An instantly uplifting chord, some shapes sound like "m7", keep 6th high up in chord.

When you get a progression of chords all with extensions, 6's, 7's, 9's and 13's etc., look for the common thread. Here keep F# as the highest note.

I	V	VI	II₇	V₇
A6	E9	F♯m7	B9	E13

A6/9   A - C♯ - E - F♯ - B

A six nine

Add the 6th and 9th notes from major scale to major triad. Strange exotic blend of sounds can link unlikely chords together.

An unusual variation on the three chord trick. Each chord weakened (or made more sophisticated) by the extensions and passing notes.

I	IV	I	V
AΔ7	D+	A6/9	E7

Asus4   A - D - E

A suspended 4th

A major triad that has the 4th note of scale 'suspended' over the 3rd. A tense sound that is resolved by releasing 4th and hearing the 3rd.

The "A sus" is, as is usual for the "sus" chord, there to provide tension and drama in an otherwise simple 2 chord progression.

I	I	I	V	I
A	Asus	A	E	Asus

A5   A - E - (A)

A5 (no 3rd) 'Power chord'

Take the 3rd out of any major/minor triad and you have a "5" chord. Most effective with loud electric playing, saves worrying about keys.

Typical minor progression. Using all "5" chords (power chords) means the melancholic aspect of minor is eliminated and you get pure grit!

I	VI	V	VII
A5	F5	E5	G5

A13   A - C♯ - E - G - B - (D) - F♯

A 13

13 chord 'should' contain all the above notes, in practice the 7th and 13th (=6th) are essential, the 9th richer, 11th unused. An exotic.

Jazzy progression that could cycle through all keys forever. Begins as classic "II", "V", "I" progression but "I" always becomes "V" so it continues...

V	I (V)	I (V)	I (V)
A13	D9	G13	C9

A+   A - C♯ - E♯

A augmented

Take a major triad and sharpen the 5th by 1 fret. Often used after the major, the sharp 5th progressing 1 fret at a time to next chord.

The augmented chord here is used to bridge between "A" and "A6" (or F#m7). To play; strum A then move E to E# then to F# to G (on A7).

I	I	I	I
A	A+	A6	A7

Am6   A - C - E - F#

A minor 6 — Add the 6th from the major scale to a minor triad. The 6th is commonly added to the triad to give a 2nd note in common with next chord.

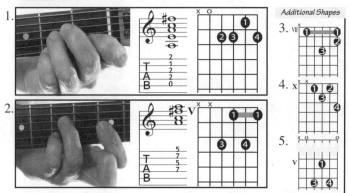

Well worn "II", "V", "I", "VI" progression. Am adds F# to become Am6 and this F# (and A) reduces impact of D as a "V" chord - effect is more relaxed.

II	V	I	VI
Am6	D	G	Em7

Am Δ7   A - C - E - G#

A minor major 7 — Add the 7th from the major scale to a minor triad. Rarely used on its own. Usually follows either "m7", "m" or "m6". Similar to augmented.

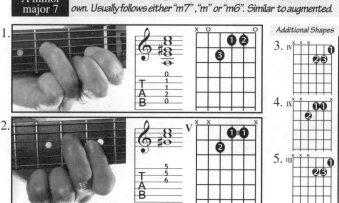

The AmΔ7 is used here simply to create intrigue and 'hold-up' the momentum of an otherwise routine progression.

II	II	II	V	IV	V	IV	I
Am	AmΔ7	AmΔ7	D	C	D	C	G

A7sus4   A - D - E - G

A7 sus 4 — With a flat (minor) 7th AND a suspended 4th this chord is over-loaded with tension. Sometimes used in place of the "11" chord.

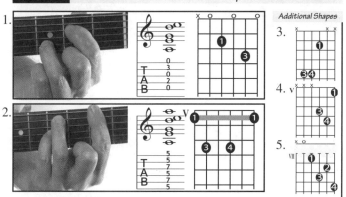

More or less a regular "II", "V", "I" progression with the "7 sus" chord resisting the resolution you normally get on the "I" chord, D2 extends the resistance.

II	V	I	IV
Bm7	E7	A7sus	D2

A7#9   A - C# - E - G - B#(=C)

A7 sharp 9 — Wickedly tense, a regular 7 chord with a sharp 9th (equal to sticking a minor 3rd on top). Usually on either 5th or 1st notes of the scale.

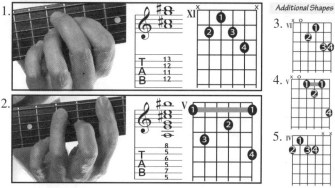

No ordinary 3 chord trick when you add "7#9" to the "I" chord. Gives it a very heavy blues flavour.

I	I	IV	V
A7#9	A7#9	D	E

Am13   A - C - E - G - B - (D) - F#

A minor 13 — "m13" 'should' contain all above notes but often omits 9th and 11th. The "m11" is also quite common and has 11th but no 13th.

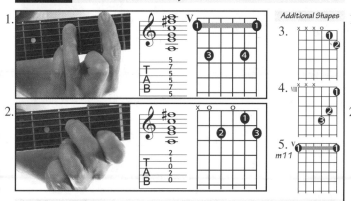

Am13 into D7 is very smooth. The "m13" is a fascinating sound and you barely notice Am13 move to D7 - common notes = smooth effect.

II	V	I	VI
Am13	D7	G	Em

A-5   A - C# - E♭

A flat 5 — Another tension chord that has a powerful need to resolve to the major chord.

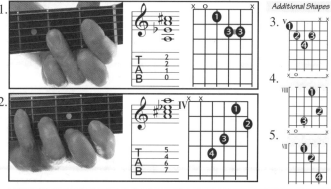

A "I", "IV", "V" common progression given a bit of sophistication by using the E (in A), Eb (in A-5) D, to smooth the progression.

I	I	IV	V
A	A-5	D	E

Bb
Bb Major

Bb - D - F

The major triad is built using the 1st, 3rd and 5th notes from the major scale. It's the building block for all major & dominant chords.

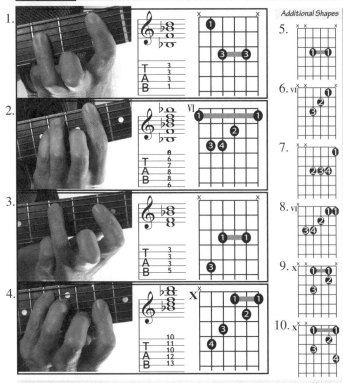

Additional Shapes

Bb major on the strong "I" position in this classic progression. What a major chord is all about.

I	VI	IV	V
Bb	Gm	Eb	F

Bb△7(9)
Bb Major 7 (Bb Major 9)

Bb - D - F - A

Add the 7th note from the major scale to the major triad. The classic 'chill out' chord, very relaxed. Add 9th note for 'more'.

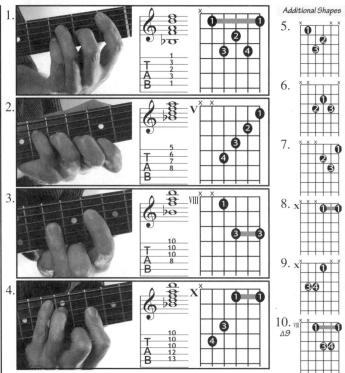

Additional Shapes

Two major seven chords played one after the other will usually be on the "I" and "IV". The effect is easy going - but it's drifting nowhere.

I	IV	I	IV
Bb△7	Eb△7	Bb△7	Eb△7

Bb7
Bb dominant 7

Bb - D - F - Ab

Add the 7th note from the minor scale to the MAJOR triad. Found mainly on the 5th note of the scale - powering back to the "I" chord.

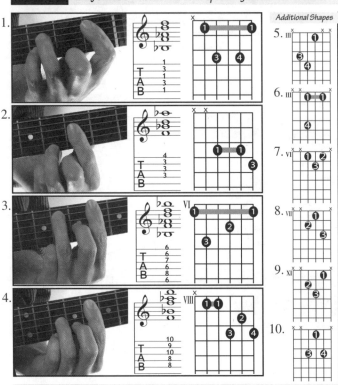

Additional Shapes

The power of a dominant 7 chord very apparent here. From the moment it starts you can hear it's going to progress to Eb.

V	IV	II	I
Bb7	Ab7	Fm	Eb

Bb9
Bb9 and Bb add9 (Bb2)

Bb - D - F - (Ab) - C

The shapes of '9' and 'add 9' are similar but the sound of the full 9 chord is jazzier than 'add 9 ', as it includes the 7th.

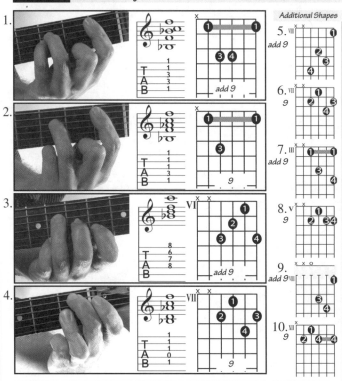

Additional Shapes

The difference between "add 9" and "dominant 9 (9)" is on show here and is fully exploited. The key is constantly shifting.

I	I	III	VII
Bb2 (add9)	Bb9	Db5	Ab5

Bbm — Bb Minor — Bb - Db - F

Bb Minor — The minor triad is built using the 1st, 3rd and 5th notes from the minor scale. It's the building block for all minor chords.

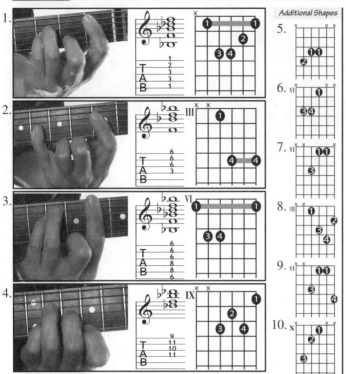

Additional Shapes

A minor "I", "IV", "V" progression where although the Bb minor is the "I", is never strong. This is because the Fm remains minor rather than "7".

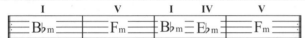

I	V	I	IV	V
Bbm	Fm	Bbm	Ebm	Fm

Bbm7 — Bb minor 7 — Bb - Db - F - Ab

Bb minor 7 — Add the 7th note from the minor scale to the minor triad. The character is milder, not so melancholic as the minor triad but is less positive.

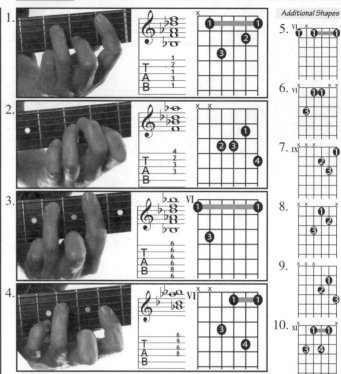

Additional Shapes

Classic 'm7' used on the "II" - especially as part of a "II", "V", "I" (the implied progression here). However, tension increases by delaying the "I".

II	V	II	III
Bbm7	Eb	Bbm7	Cm7

Bbm9 — Bbm9 and Bbm add9 (Bbm2) — Bb - Db - F - (Ab) - C

The shapes of 'm9' and 'm add 9' are similar but the sound of the 'm add9' chord is more 'mystic' than 'm9', as it omits the 7th.

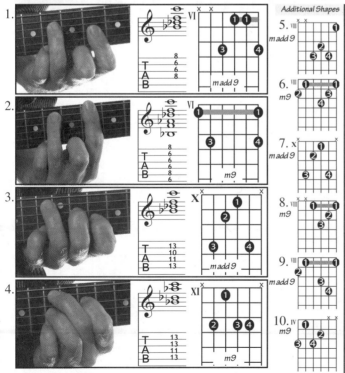

Additional Shapes

A regular progression using all "m9's". The character of the chord is apparent but keeping 9th on Fm prevents progression from resolving.

IV	V	I	I
Bbm9	Cm9	Fm9	Fm9

Bbº — diminished group — Bbº, Bbº7 & Bbm7b5 — Bb - Db - Fb - (Ab(Abb))

Diminished chords have similar fingerings and uses, the m7b5 adds a minor 7th and for º7 flatten the minor 7th another fret.

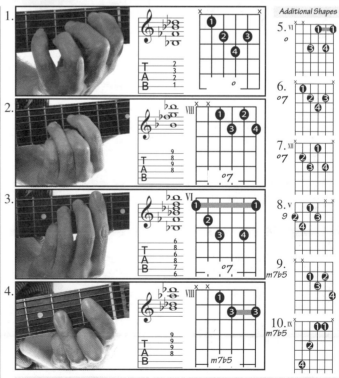

Additional Shapes

Bbº is used to link A with Bm7. Bº is best thought of here as "A" with the root raised by a semitone (1 fret). "A" - "A#" - "B".

I	I#r	II	V
A	Bbº	Bm7	E9

Bb/A#

Bb6 — Bb - D - F - G
Bb Six — Add the sixth note of the major scale to the major triad. An instantly uplifting chord, some shapes sound like "m7", keep 6th high up in chord.

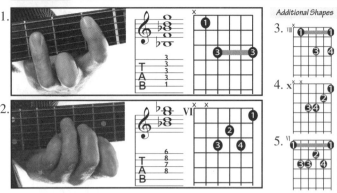

Six chords always sound optimistic. Also, adding the "G" increases the number of common notes between the "Bb" & "Eb" chords - smoother.

I	IV	I	V
Bb6	Eb	Bb6	F6

Bb6/9 — Bb - D - F - G - C
Bb six nine — Add the 6th and 9th notes from major scale to major triad. Strange exotic blend of sounds can link unlikely chords together.

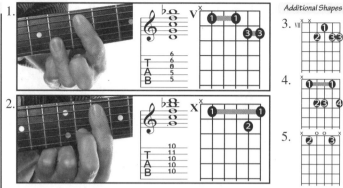

Shows the jazzier side of the 6/9 chord and makes an interesting sound out of a basic "IV", "V", "IV", "I" progression.

IV	V	IV	I
Bb6/9	C9	Bb6/9	F6

Bbsus4 — Bb - Eb - F
Bb suspended 4th — A major triad that has the 4th note of scale 'suspended' over the 3rd. A tense sound that is resolved by releasing 4th and hearing the 3rd.

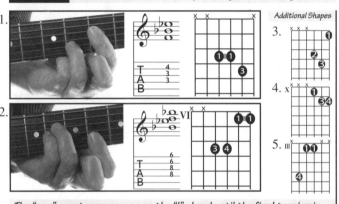

The "sus" creates suspense on the "I" chord until the final tension in "F7" takes us back for more.

I	I	I	V
Bbsus	Bb	Bb9	F7

Bb5 — Bb - F - (Bb)
Bb5 (no 3rd) 'Power chord' — Take the 3rd out of any major/minor triad and you have a "5" chord. Most effective with loud electric playing, saves worrying about keys.

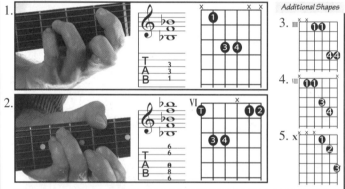

With the two opening chords a tone (2 frets) apart, it's obvious that you're hearing "IV" and "V" chords, the drop to F, the "I", is inevitable.

IV	V	IV	I
Bb5	C5	Bb5	F5

Bb13 — Bb - D - F - Ab - C - (Eb) - G
Bb 13 — 13 chord 'should' contain all the above notes, in practice the 7th and 13th (=6th) are essential, the 9th richer, 11th unused. An exotic.

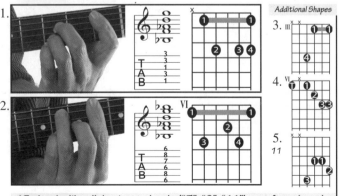

13 chords, like all dominant chords ("7", "9", "11") are often the only chords. However, changing chord always means changing key - bluesy.

I	I	IV	IV
Bb13	Bb13	Eb13	Eb13

Bb+ — Bb - D - F#
Bb augmented — Take a major triad and sharpen the 5th by 1 fret. Often used after the major, the sharp 5th progressing 1 fret at a time to next chord.

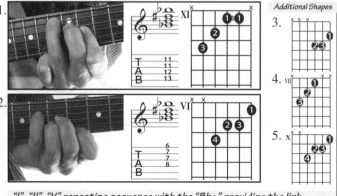

"I", "II", "V" repeating sequence with the "Bb+" providing the link between "Bb" and "C". The relevant notes to play are "F", "F#" and "G".

I	I	II	V
Bb	Bb+	Cm	F

Bbm6   Bb - Db - F - G

Bb minor six — Add the 6th from the major scale to a minor triad. The 6th is commonly added to the triad to give a 2nd note in common with next chord.

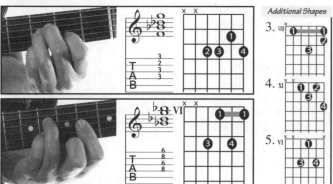

Bbm to C in the key of G would be rather odd but add a "G" to the Bbm and this common note makes sense of the chord change and sounds amazing.

bIII	IV	I	VI
Bbm6	C	G	Em7

Bbm△7   Bb - Db - F - A

Bb minor major 7 — Add the 7th from the major scale to a minor triad. Rarely used on its own. Usually follows either "m7", "m" or "m6". Similar to augmented.

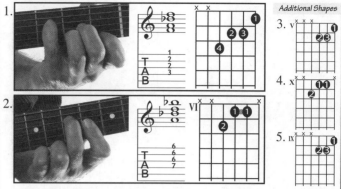

"Bbm△7" is used as a link from "Bbm" to "Ab". Make prominent the scalar drop "Bb" - "A" - "Ab". This is the most common use for "m△7".

II	II	I	V
Bbm	Bbm△7	Ab	Eb

Bb7sus4   Bb - Eb - F - Ab

Bb seven suspended 4th — With a flat (minor) 7th AND a suspended 4th this chord is overloaded with tension. Sometimes used in place of the "11" chord.

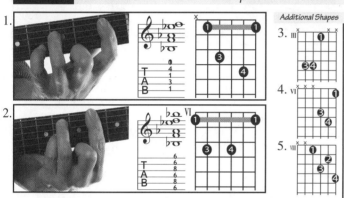

Routine chord progression given extra interest by adding "7 sus 4" to the "V" chord which makes you look forward even more to resolution on the "I".

I	V	IV	V
Eb	Bb7sus Bb	Ab	Bb7sus

Bb7#9   Bb - D - F - Ab - C#

Bb seven sharp 9th — Wickedly tense, a regular 7 chord with a sharp 9th (equal to sticking a minor 3rd on top). Usually on either 5th or 1st notes of the scale.

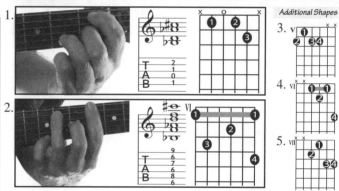

The "7#9" chord is positioned on the flattened sixth degree which is the dominant 7 chord raised a fret, moves to A7 - the "I" is almost irrelevant.

#V	V	#V	I
Bb7#9	A7	Bb7#9	D

Bbm13   Bb - Db - F - Ab - C - (Eb) - G

Bb minor 13 — "m13" 'should' contain all above notes but often omits 9th and 11th. The "m11" is also quite common and has 11th but no 13th.

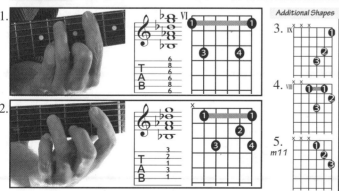

The Bb13 uses the 13 as an 'extra' hanging note, rather than for common ground between chords. Less common, more interesting.

V	VII	IV	I
Bbm13	Db7	Abm13	Ebm7

Bb-5   Bb - D - Fb

Bb Flat 5 — Another tension chord that has a powerful need to resolve to the major chord.

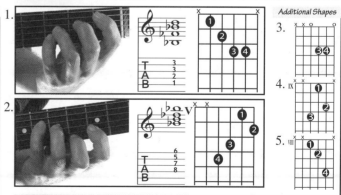

The flat 5 here is used to 'manufacture' a leading tone to "F" which makes the change more interesting. It is also more tense.

I	IV	IV	I	V
F	Bb	Bb-5	F	C

B

B — B Major
B - D♯ - F♯

The major triad is built using the 1st, 3rd and 5th notes from the major scale. It's the building block for all major & dominant chords.

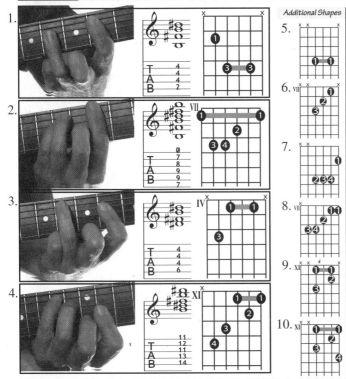

Additional Shapes
5. 6. 7. 8. 9. 10.

Although "B" is a major chord on the "I", it has to fight to take charge, as the chord extensions on the other chords smooth and weaken it.

I	IV	V	II
B	E△7	F♯6	C♯m add9

B△7(9) — B Major 7 (B Major 9)
B - D♯ - F♯ - A♯ - (C♯)

Add the 7th note from the major scale to the major triad. The classic 'chill out' chord, very relaxed. Add 9th note for 'more'.

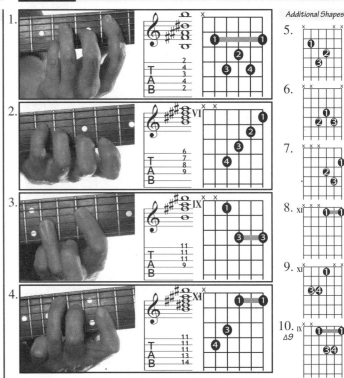

Additional Shapes
5. 6. 7. 8. 9. 10. △9

The major 7 chord is sometimes used to 'bridge' a major chord and the "7" chord with the same root. So you hear "B", "A♯", A in the melody.

I	I	I	V
B	B△7	B7	F♯

B7 — B dominant 7
B - D♯ - F♯ - A

Add the 7th note from the minor scale to the MAJOR triad. Found mainly on the 5th note of the scale - powering back to the "i" chord.

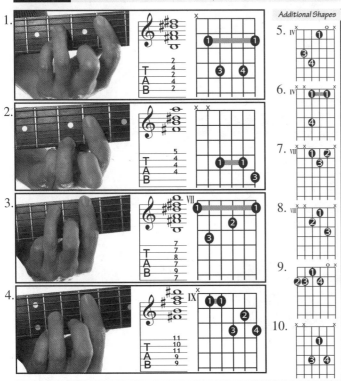

Additional Shapes
5. 6. 7. 8. 9. 10.

The classic minor progression where "B7" is heard in the "7" chords' most decisive role as "V" chord of a minor key - gives serious power to key note "E".

I	VII	VI	V7
Em	D	C	B7

B9 — B9 and B add9 (B2)
B - D♯ - F♯ - (A) - C♯

The shapes of '9' and 'add 9' are similar but the sound of the full 9 chord is jazzier than 'add 9', as it includes the 7th.

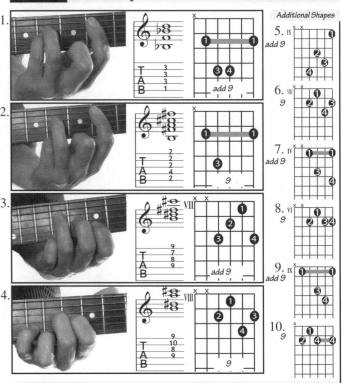

Additional Shapes
5. add 9   6. 9   7. add 9   8. 9   9. add 9   10. 9

Solid minor progression - the added "9" (C♯) keeps this note hanging on from the "I" & "IV" chords. "C♯" is maintained throughout for stability.

I	IV	VII	V
C♯m	F♯5	Badd9	G♯sus

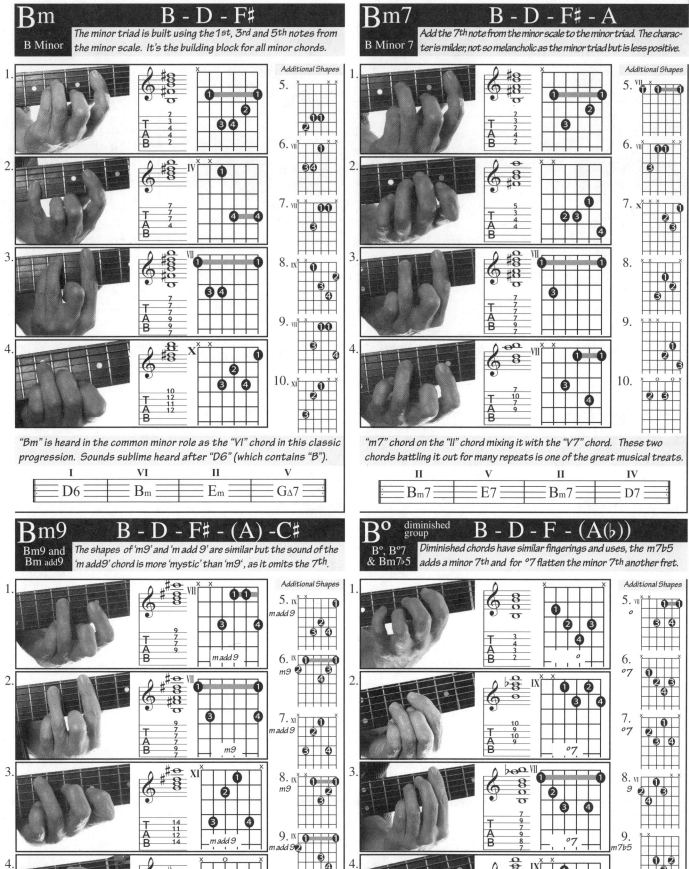

Bm — B Minor — B - D - F#

The minor triad is built using the 1st, 3rd and 5th notes from the minor scale. It's the building block for all minor chords.

"Bm" is heard in the common minor role as the "VI" chord in this classic progression. Sounds sublime heard after "D6" (which contains "B").

I	VI	II	V
D6	Bm	Em	GΔ7

Bm7 — B Minor 7 — B - D - F# - A

Add the 7th note from the minor scale to the minor triad. The character is milder, not so melancholic as the minor triad but is less positive.

"m7" chord on the "II" chord mixing it with the "V7" chord. These two chords battling it out for many repeats is one of the great musical treats.

II	V	II	IV
Bm7	E7	Bm7	D7

Bm9 — Bm9 and Bm add9 — B - D - F# - (A) - C#

The shapes of 'm9' and 'm add 9' are similar but the sound of the 'm add9' chord is more 'mystic' than 'm9', as it omits the 7th.

Bm9 in the weak "III" position adds a "C#" which should help lead to "D", but really only introduces a key change which is interesting but weak.

III	V	II	IV	V
Bm9	D	Am9	C	D

B° — diminished group — B°, B°7 & Bm7♭5 — B - D - F - (A(♭))

Diminished chords have similar fingerings and uses, the m7b5 adds a minor 7th and for °7 flatten the minor 7th another fret.

Like a permanent ending (or cadence) when the "F" in "B°" leads up to "F#" at the same time "B" moves down to ""A#".

I	V	VII	V
B°	F#	A°7	E

15

B

B6 B - D♯ - F♯ - G♯
B six

Add the sixth note of the major scale to the major triad. An instantly uplifting chord, some shapes sound like "m7", keep 6th high up in chord.

Additional Shapes

Unusual role for "B6" as the "VII" chord in a minor progression - the added "G#" is helping foretell the "I" chord as well as sliding silkily into "Eb7".

VII	II (V)	(I) V	I
B6	Eb7	Ab7	C♯m7

B6/9 B - D♯ - F♯ - G♯ - C♯
B six nine

Add the 6th and 9th notes from major scale to major triad. Strange exotic blend of sounds can link unlikely chords together.

Additional Shapes

A really sophisticated "IV"-"V"-"I". By adding "C#" and "G#" to the "B major triad 2 more notes found in "C#9" are embedded in the "B" chord.

IV	V	IV	I
B6/9	C♯9	B6/9	F♯6

Bsus4 B - E - F♯
B suspended 4th

A major triad that has the 4th note of scale 'suspended' over the 3rd. A tense sound that is resolved by releasing 4th and hearing the 3rd.

Additional Shapes

One of the best ways to liven up the good old 3 chord trick of "I"-"IV"-"V" is to introduce the "sus4" to any "I", IV and V chords.

I		I		IV	V
Bsus	B	Bsus	B	E	F♯sus F♯

B5 B - F♯ - (B)
B5 (no 3rd) 'Power chord'

Take the 3rd out of any major/minor triad and you have a "5" chord. Most effective with loud electric playing, saves worrying about keys.

Additional Shapes

Only one way to create an aggressive chord progression that descends 'Batman'-like, i.e. in semitones (1 fret) is to use chords with no 3rd's or extensions.

I	VII	♭VII	VII
B5	B♭5	A5	B♭5

B13 B - D♯ - F♯ - A - C♯ - (E) - G♯
B 13

13 chord 'should' contain all the above notes, in practice the 7th and 13th (=6th) are essential, the 9th richer, 11th unused. An exotic.

Additional Shapes

A jazzy "V" chord on an otherwise fairly routine progression. Glides effortlessly into "E" chord. Note "+" chord moving back to "B".

V	I	VI	VI♭r
B13	E	C♯m7	C+

B+ B - D♯ - F♯♯ (=G)
B augmented (or B sharp 5)

Take a major triad and sharpen the 5th by 1 fret. Often used after the major, the sharp 5th progressing 1 fret at a time to next chord.

Additional Shapes

The augmented chord has two main roles, either as a 'cliff-hanger' note, or as a bridging chord - here the latter, listen for "F#" (in B)", "G" (in B+), "G#" (in E).

I	I	V	V
E	E7	B	B+

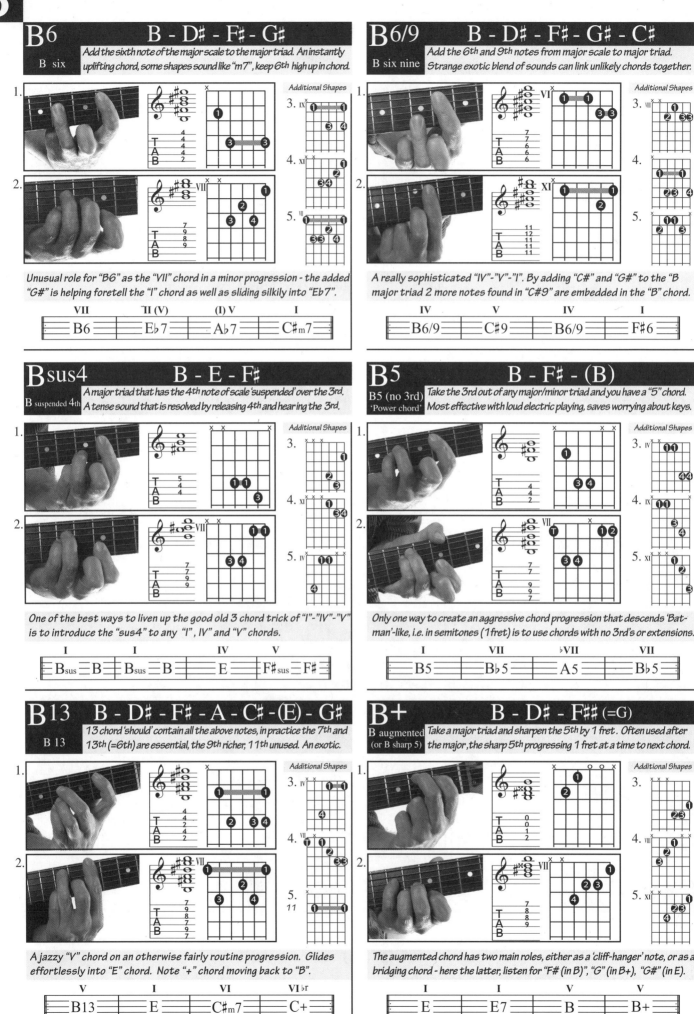

Bm6   B - D - F# - G#

B minor 6 — Add the 6th from the major scale to a minor triad. The 6th is commonly added to the triad to give a 2nd note in common with next chord.

A classic progression has been significantly disguised and tamed by adding a 6th to the "II" chord. The "G#" carries continuity into the "E".

II	V	I	I
Bm6	E	A	A6

Bm∆7   B - D - F# - A#

B minor major 7 — Add the 7th from the major scale to a minor triad. Rarely used on its own. Usually follows either "m7", "m" or "m6". Similar to augmented.

Famous use of the "m∆7" to bridge the "m7" chord to the pure minor chord (same root). Listen for "A"-"A#"-"B"-"A#".

I	I	I	I
Bm7	Bm∆7	Bm	Bm∆7

B7sus4   B - E - F# - A

B7 sus 4 — With a flat (minor) 7th AND a suspended 4th this chord is overloaded with tension. Sometimes used in place of the "11" chord.

The "7sus4" not usually so unassuming as here. Especially tamed if the exact same "E" from "F#m7" is retained by "B7sus4".

II	V	I	I
F#m7	B7sus	E∆7	E∆7

B7#9   B - D# - F# - A - C## (=D)

B7 sharp 9 — Wickedly tense, a regular 7 chord with a sharp 9th (equal to sticking a minor 3rd on top). Usually on either 5th or 1st notes of the scale.

Looks like it'll never work but... the "D" links "B7#9" and "Bb7", which is itself a raised "V" chord that slides back to 'correct' "A7" and so to "Dm" (I).

VI#r	VI	V	I
B7#9	Bb7	A7	Dm

Bm13   B - D - F# - A - C# - (E) - G#

B minor 13 — "m13" should' contain all above notes but often omits 9th and 11th. The "m11" is also quite common and has 11th but no 13th.

Dressing up the "II" chord in a common "II"-"V"-"I" progression disguises and smooths the progression.

II	V	I	V	VI
Bm13	E	A	E	F#m

B-5   B - D# - F

B flat 5 — Another tension chord that has a powerful need to resolve to the major chord.

Flattening the 5th usually progresses the 5th to the root of the next chord, i.e. "F#"-"F"-"E". Here you're teased and it goes back to "F#".

I	I	I	IV
B	B-5	B	E

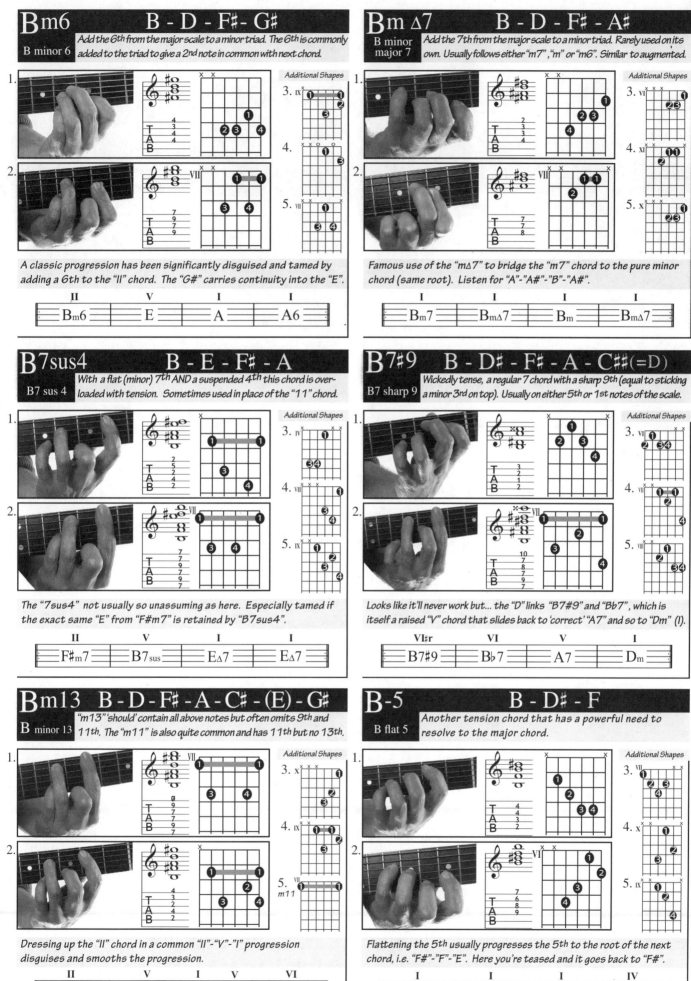

Additional Shapes

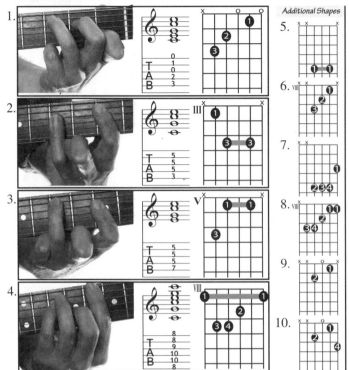

C

C — C - E - G

C Major

The major triad is built using the 1st, 3rd and 5th notes from the major scale. It's the building block for all major & dominant chords.

1. 2. 3. 4.

Additional Shapes
5. 6. 7. 8. VIII 9. 10.

The "C" chord in the major chords most powerful role as the "I" chord, amazingly powerful (and much used) progression.

I	V	VI	V
C	G	Am	G

CΔ7(9) — C - E - G - B- (D)

C Major 7
(C Major 9)

Add the 7th note from the major scale to the major triad. The classic 'chill out' chord, very relaxed. Add 9th note for 'more'.

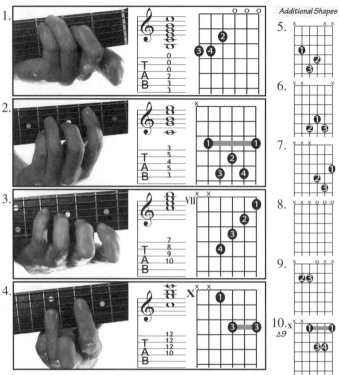

1. 2. 3. 4.

Additional Shapes
5. 6. 7. 8. 9. 10.x Δ9

The classic "II"-"V"-"I" progression in it's jazzy form with most of the chord extensions. The "I" chord will always be "Δ7" or "Δ9".

II	V	I	1
Dm7	G	CΔ7	CΔ9

C7 — C - E - G - B♭

C dominant 7

Add the 7th note from the minor scale to the MAJOR triad. Found mainly on the 5th note of the scale - powering back to the "I" chord.

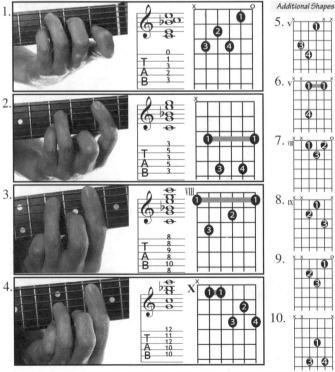

1. 2. 3. 4.

Additional Shapes
5. v 6. v 7. VIII 8. IX 9. 10.

Even though the "C7" follows the "C" major chord it sounds like a key change and in fact is progressing from "C" to "F" and then "F minor".

I	I	IV	IV
C	C7	F7	Fm

C9 — C - E - G - (B) - D

C9 and
C add9 (C2)

The shapes of '9' and 'add 9' are similar but the sound of the full 9 chord is jazzier than 'add 9', as it includes the 7th.

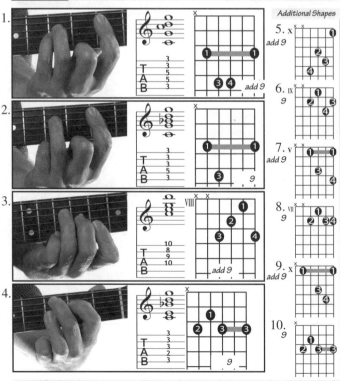

1. 2. 3. 4.

Additional Shapes
5. x add 9 6. IX 9 7. v add 9 8. VII 9 9. x add 9 10. 9

The classic "II"-"V"-"I" progression in very jazzy, smooth mode. Using "C9" rather than "major" or "7" increases shared notes - smoother.

II	V	I	I
Gm7	C9	FΔ7	F

18

Cm — C - Eb - G
C Minor

The minor triad is built using the 1st, 3rd and 5th notes from the minor scale. It's the building block for all minor chords.

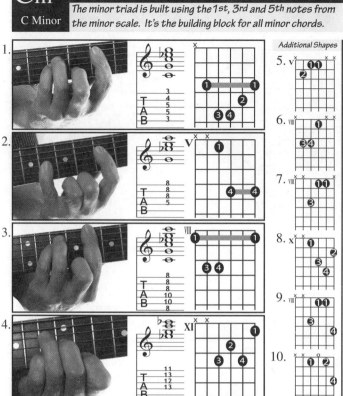

Additional Shapes: 5. 6. 7. 8. 9. 10.

The "Cm" looks like it should be at the head of a strong minor progression but the final "Bb" pushes the key towards "Eb" so "Cm" is left weak sounding.

I	IV	V	bVII
Cm	Fm	Gm	Bb

Cm7 — C - Eb - G - Bb
C Minor 7

Add the 7th note from the minor scale to the minor triad. The character is milder, not so melancholic as the minor triad but is less positive.

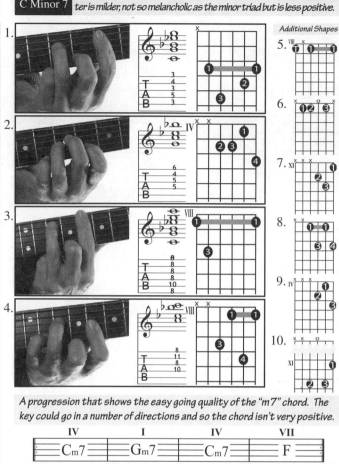

Additional Shapes: 5. 6. 7. 8. 9. 10.

A progression that shows the easy going quality of the "m7" chord. The key could go in a number of directions and so the chord isn't very positive.

IV	I	IV	VII
Cm7	Gm7	Cm7	F

Cm9 — C - Eb - G - (Bb) - D
Cm9 and Cm add9

The shapes of 'm9' and 'm add 9' are similar but the sound of the 'm add9' chord is more 'mystic' than 'm9', as it omits the 7th.

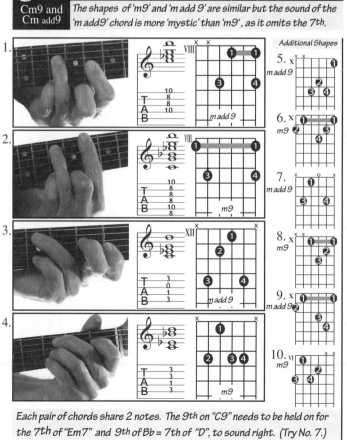

Additional Shapes: 5. 6. 7. 8. 9. 10.

Each pair of chords share 2 notes. The 9th on "C9" needs to be held on for the 7th of "Em7" and 9th of Bb = 7th of "D", to sound right. (Try No. 7.)

V	#III	IV	II
Cm9	Em7	Bbm9	Dm7

C° — diminished group — C - Eb - Gb - (Bb(bb))
C°, C°7 & Cm7b5

Diminished chords have similar fingerings and uses, the m7b5 adds a minor 7th and for °7 flatten the minor 7th another fret.

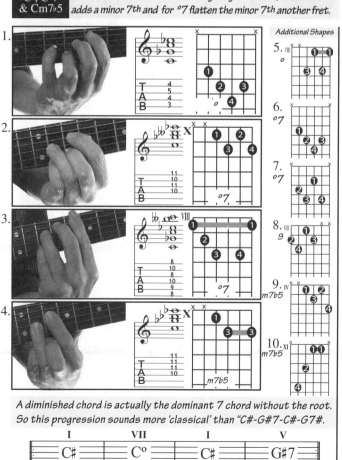

Additional Shapes: 5. 6. 7. 8. 9. 10.

A diminished chord is actually the dominant 7 chord without the root. So this progression sounds more 'classical' than "C#-G#7-C#-G7#".

I	VII	I	V
C#	C°	C#	G#7

19

C

C6 — C - E - G - A
C six
Add the sixth note of the major scale to the major triad. An instantly uplifting chord, some shapes sound like "m7", keep 6th high up in chord.

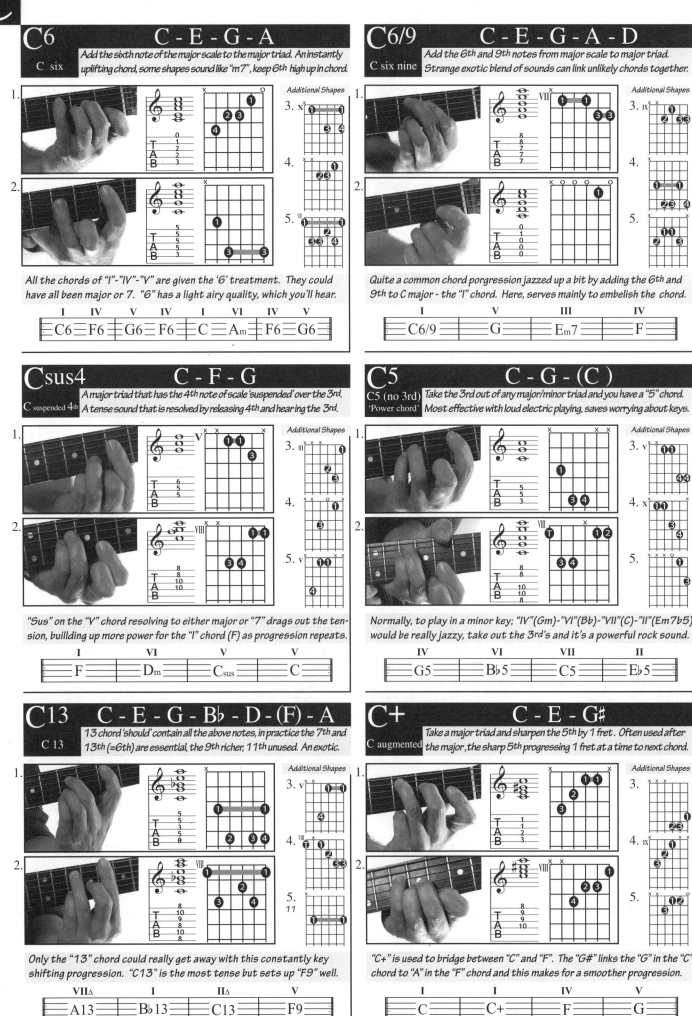

Additional Shapes
3. 4. 5.

All the chords of "I"-"IV"-"V" are given the '6' treatment. They could have all been major or 7. "6" has a light airy quality, which you'll hear.

I	IV	V	IV	I	VI	IV	V
C6	F6	G6	F6	C	Am	F6	G6

C6/9 — C - E - G - A - D
C six nine
Add the 6th and 9th notes from major scale to major triad. Strange exotic blend of sounds can link unlikely chords together.

Additional Shapes
3. 4. 5.

Quite a common chord porgression jazzed up a bit by adding the 6th and 9th to C major - the "I" chord. Here, serves mainly to embelish the chord.

I	V	III	IV
C6/9	G	Em7	F

Csus4 — C - F - G
C suspended 4th
A major triad that has the 4th note of scale 'suspended' over the 3rd. A tense sound that is resolved by releasing 4th and hearing the 3rd.

Additional Shapes
3. 4. 5.

"Sus" on the "V" chord resolving to either major or "7" drags out the tension, buillding up more power for the "I" chord (F) as progression repeats.

I	VI	V	V
F	Dm	Csus	C

C5 — C - G - (C)
C5 (no 3rd)
'Power chord'
Take the 3rd out of any major/minor triad and you have a "5" chord. Most effective with loud electric playing, saves worrying about keys.

Additional Shapes
3. 4. 5.

Normally, to play in a minor key; "IV"(Gm)-"VI"(Bb)-"VII"(C)-"II"(Em7b5) would be really jazzy, take out the 3rd's and it's a powerful rock sound.

IV	VI	VII	II
G5	Bb5	C5	Eb5

C13 — C - E - G - Bb - D - (F) - A
C 13
13 chord 'should' contain all the above notes, in practice the 7th and 13th (=6th) are essential, the 9th richer, 11th unused. An exotic.

Additional Shapes
3. 4. 5.

Only the "13" chord could really get away with this constantly key shifting progression. "C13" is the most tense but sets up "F9" well.

VIIΔ	I	IIΔ	V
A13	Bb13	C13	F9

C+ — C - E - G#
C augmented
Take a major triad and sharpen the 5th by 1 fret. Often used after the major, the sharp 5th progressing 1 fret at a time to next chord.

Additional Shapes
3. 4. 5.

"C+" is used to bridge between "C" and "F". The "G#" links the "G" in the "C" chord to "A" in the "F" chord and this makes for a smoother progression.

I	I	IV	V
C	C+	F	G

Cm6 — C - E♭ - G - A

C minor 6
Add the 6th from the major scale to a minor triad. The 6th is commonly added to the triad to give a 2nd note in common with next chord.

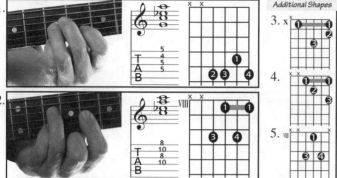

Additional Shapes
3.
4.
5.

"Cm"-"A♭"-"Cm"-"G7" is quite a strong minor progression. The addition of "A" to the Cm creates a key change and gives a chromatic feel to the implied melody.

I	VI	I	V
Cm6	A♭	Cm6	G7

Cm Δ7 — C - E♭ - G - B

C minor major 7
Add the 7th from the major scale to a minor triad. Rarely used on its own. Usually follows either "m7", "m" or "m6". Similar to augmented.

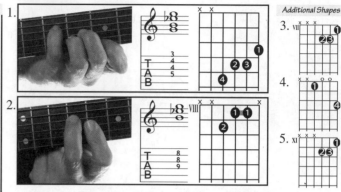

Additional Shapes
3.
4.
5.

"mΔ7" is a common 'bridge' chord. In this example the notes "C" and "B♭" are linked by the "B" in "CmΔ7". Simple but effective.

IV	I	I	VII	I	I (V)
Fm	Cm	CmΔ7	B♭	Cm	C

C7sus4 — C - F - G - B♭

C7 sus 4
With a flat (minor) 7th AND a suspended 4th this chord is over-loaded with tension. Sometimes used in place of the "11" chord.

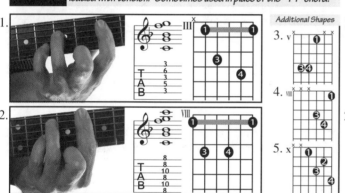

Additional Shapes
3.
4.
5.

Although a standard 3 chord trick the "7sus4" chords stretch out the tension - it is also melodic implying "F"(C7sus)-"E"(C7)-D(B♭) etc.

I	V	V		V	
F	C7sus	C7	B♭	C7sus	C7

C7#9 — C - E - G - B♭ - D#

C7 sharp 9
Wickedly tense, a regular 7 chord with a sharp 9th (equal to sticking a minor 3rd on top). Usually on either 5th or 1st notes of the scale.

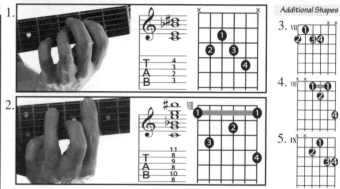

Additional Shapes
3.
4.
5.

A "V"-"IV"-"I" progression is one of the most well worn paths in music - however, stick a "#9" on the "V7" and it's anything but dull.

V	V	IV	I
C7#9	C7#9	B♭	F

Cm13 — C - E♭ - G - B♭ - D - (F) - A

C minor 13
"m13" 'should' contain all above notes but often omits 9th and 11th. The "m11" is also quite common and has 11th but no 13th.

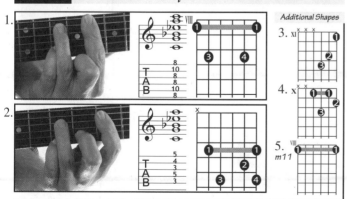

Additional Shapes
3.
4.
5. m11

An unusual way of dressing up a minor "I"-"V"-"IV" progression. For this to sound good, the chords need to use extensions to create a logical melody.

I	V	IV	V
Cm13	G7	Fm13	G7

C-5 — C - E - G♭

C flat 5
Another tension chord that has a powerful need to resolve to the major chord.

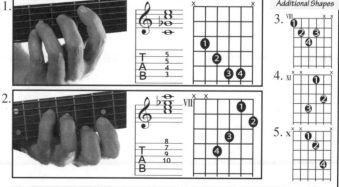

Additional Shapes
3.
4.
5.

A simple and well used progression would normally be "G"-"Em"-"C"-"D". However, the C-5 is an interesting substitute for "D".

I	VI	IV	I
G	Em	C-5	G

C#/Db

C# — C# Major — C# - E# - G#

The major triad is built using the 1st, 3rd and 5th notes from the major scale. It's the building block for all major & dominant chords.

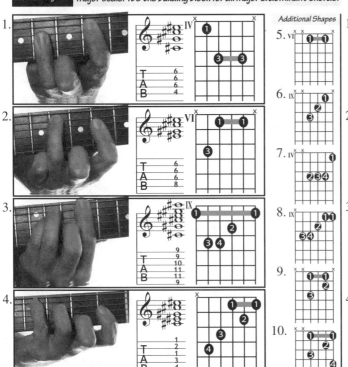

Additional Shapes

This progression is totally predictable except, instead of going to "G#" on bar 4 it goes to "F#" and then repeats. This has the effect of weakening the "C#".

I	IV	VI	IV
C#	F#	B♭m (=A#m)	F#

C#Δ7(9) — C# Major 7 (C# Major 9) — C# - E# - G#- B# (D#)

Add the 7th note from the major scale to the major triad. The classic 'chill out' chord, very relaxed. Add 9th note for 'more'.

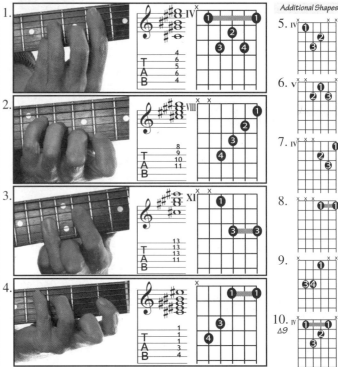

Additional Shapes

A progression that is neither very predictable nor strange. The tension in the "IV" chord isn't fully resolved by "C#Δ7" - as you'd expect.

IV	I	IV	II
F#	C#Δ7	F#	D#m (=E♭m)

C#7 — C# Dominant 7 — C# - E# - G#- B

Add the 7th note from the minor scale to the MAJOR triad. Found mainly on the 5th note of the scale - powering back to the "I" chord.

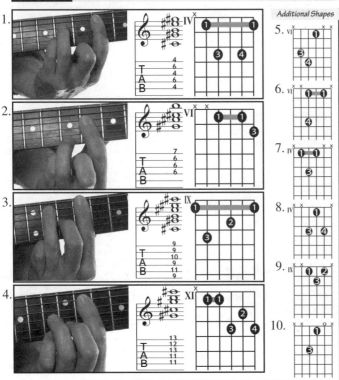

Additional Shapes

A strong minor progression that is slightly off the normal route for these chords - however, the "C#7" ("V7") is so strong it pulls all back together.

I	IV	VI	V
F#m	Bm	D	C#7

C#9 — C# 9 and C# add9 (C#2) — C# - E# - G# - (B)- D#

The shapes of '9' and 'add 9' are similar but the sound of the full 9 chord is jazzier than 'add 9 ', as it includes the 7th.

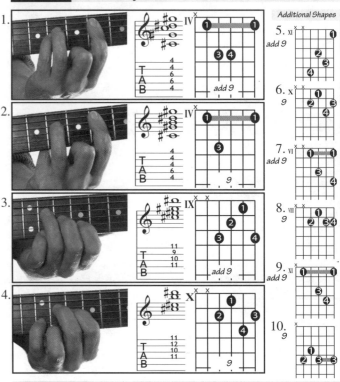

Additional Shapes

A bluesy, jazzy 3 chord trick. Using "C#9" on the "IV" chord means the key changes, blues fashion. The 9th of "C#7" (D#) is common to "G#" = slick.

I	IV	I	IV	V
G#	C#9	G#	C#9	D#9

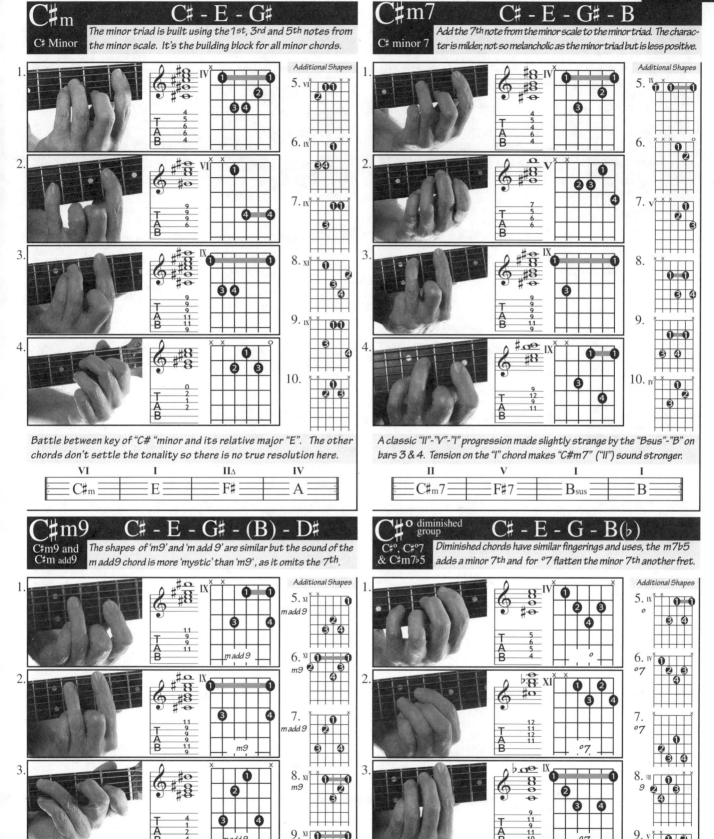

C#m — C# - E - G#

C# Minor — The minor triad is built using the 1st, 3rd and 5th notes from the minor scale. It's the building block for all minor chords.

Additional Shapes

Battle between key of "C#" minor and its relative major "E". The other chords don't settle the tonality so there is no true resolution here.

VI	I	II△	IV
C#m	E	F#	A

C#m7 — C# - E - G# - B

C# minor 7 — Add the 7th note from the minor scale to the minor triad. The character is milder, not so melancholic as the minor triad but is less positive.

Additional Shapes

A classic "II"-"V"-"I" progression made slightly strange by the "Bsus"-"B" on bars 3 & 4. Tension on the "I" chord makes "C#m7" ("II") sound stronger.

II	V	I	I
C#m7	F#7	Bsus	B

C#m9 — C# - E - G# - (B) - D#

C#m9 and C#m add9 — The shapes of 'm9' and 'm add 9' are similar but the sound of the m add9 chord is more 'mystic' than 'm9', as it omits the 7th.

Additional Shapes

Adding the "9" to "C#m" means that notes converge on "A" from both directions. "B" moves to "A" and "G#" to "A" ("C# & E" are constant) = powerful.

I	VI	I	IV
C#m add9	A	C#m add9	F#m7

C#° diminished group — C# - E - G - B(b)

C#°, C#°7 & C#m7b5 — Diminished chords have similar fingerings and uses, the m7b5 adds a minor 7th and for °7 flatten the minor 7th another fret.

Additional Shapes

3 chord trick suiting jazzy blues style. Most common use of diminished chord is linking the "IV" & "V" chords by raising root of "IV" chord 1 fret; C-E-G to C#-E-G.

I	IV	I#r	V
G7	C7	C#°	D

23

C♯6 — C♯ - E♯ - G♯ - A♯

C♯ Six — Add the sixth note of the major scale to the major triad. An instantly uplifting chord, some shapes sound like "m7", keep 6th high up in chord.

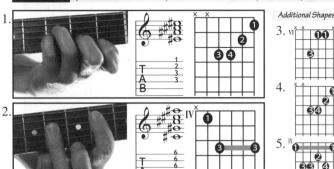

Additional Shapes

A variation on the 3 chord trick, adding the "6" is an effect rather than needed to bind chords together. The effect lightens the whole sequence.

I	V	I	IV	I	V
C♯6	G♯	C♯6	F♯	C♯6	G♯6

C♯6/9 — C♯ - E♯ - G♯ - A♯ - D♯

C♯ six nine — Add the 6th and 9th notes from major scale to major triad. Strange exotic blend of sounds can link unlikely chords together.

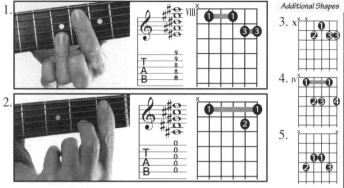

Additional Shapes

The classic "I"-"IV"-"II"-"V" progression in heavy disguise; "C6/9" & "F♯13" share so many notes that they virtually blend into one another.

I	IV	II	V
C♯6/9	F♯13	D♯m	G♯7

C♯sus4 — C♯ - F♯ - G♯

C♯ suspended 4th — A major triad that has the 4th note of scale 'suspended' over the 3rd. A tense sound that is resolved by releasing 4th and hearing the 3rd.

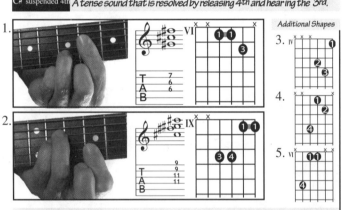

Additional Shapes

A sophisticated variation on what's basically a minor "I"-"VII"-"II"-"V". The "C♯sus" is used subtly and maintains chromatic progression yet restores original key.

I	♯VII	VII	II	V
E♭m7	DΔ7	D♭sus(C♯)	F7♭5	B♭7

C♯5 — C♯ - G♯ - (C♯)

C♯5 (no 3rd) — Take the 3rd out of any major/minor triad and you have a "5" chord. **'Power chord'** — Most effective with loud electric playing, saves worrying about keys.

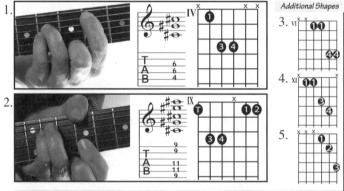

Additional Shapes

"C♯5" begins a progression that contains a strident key change. Using all power chords makes this easy to get away with.

IV	I	♭V	♭III
C♯5	G♯5	D5	B5

C♯13 — C♯ - E♯ - G♯ - B - D♯ - (F♯) - A♯

C♯ 13 — 13 chord 'should' contain all the above notes, in practice the 7th and 13th (=6th) are essential, the 9th richer, 11th unused. An exotic.

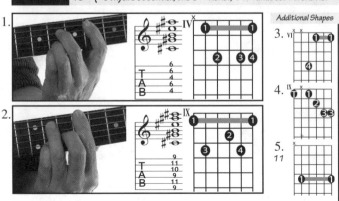

Additional Shapes

A classic chord progression given the jazz treatment. Using dominant (13) chords on "I", "IV" & "V" means the key changes on these chords - blues style.

I	V	VI	IV
C♯13	G♯13	A♯m	F♯13

C♯+ — C♯ - E♯ - G♯♯ (=A)

C♯ Augmented — Take a major triad and sharpen the 5th by 1 fret. Often used after the major, the sharp 5th progressing 1 fret at a time to next chord.

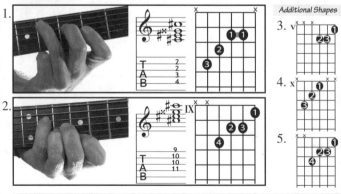

Additional Shapes

The augmented chord is commonly heard linking a major chord with a "6" chord (same root) You should hear; "G♯"(C♯)-"A"(C♯+)-"A♯"(C♯6)-"A♯"(C♯+) when played.

I	I	I	I
C♯	C♯+	C♯6	C♯+

C#m6   C# - E - G# - A#

C# minor six — Add the 6th from the major scale to a minor triad. The 6th is commonly added to the triad to give a 2nd note in common with next chord.

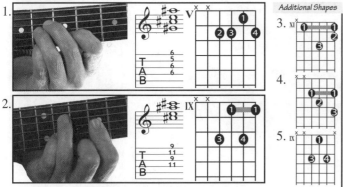

Additional Shapes

A fairly common progression where adding the "6" to C# minor in particular creates much more sophisticated voice leading, i.e "A#" (C#m6) to "B "(E).

VI	I	II	I
C#m6	E	F#m6	E2 (Eadd9)

C#m Δ7   C# - E - G# - B# (=C)

C# minor major 7 — Add the 7th from the major scale to a minor triad. Rarely used on its own. Usually follows either "m7", "m" or "m6". Similar to augmented.

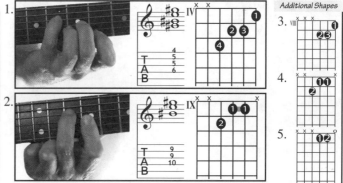

Additional Shapes

A relaxing chord sequence that uses the 'mΔ7' to make, what would otherwise be 3 bars of C#m, more interesting.

II	II	II	V
C#m	C#mΔ7	C#m	F#7

C#7sus4   C# - F# - G# - B

C# seven suspended 4th — With a flat (minor) 7th AND a suspended 4th this chord is overloaded with tension. Sometimes used in place of the "11" chord.

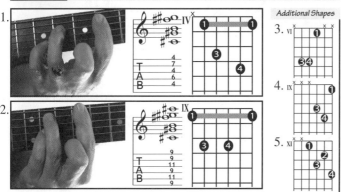

Additional Shapes

A slight variation of the 3 chord trick. The "C#7 sus4" to "C#7" is dramatic and turns "C#7" into a "V" chord to power onto "F#". G#7 restores the true key.

I	I	I	IV	V	V
C#	C#7sus	C#7	F#	G#7sus	G#7

C#7#9   C# - E# - G# - B - D## (=E)

C# seven sharp nine — Wickedly tense, a regular 7 chord with a sharp 9th (equal to sticking a minor 3rd on top). Usually on either 5th or 1st notes of the scale.

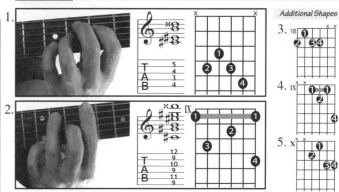

Additional Shapes

The 3 chord trick made dramatic by turning "C#" temporarily into the "V" chord. This progression goes one step further by adding the "#9".

V	I	I	IV
G#	C#	C#7#9	F#

C#m13   C# - E - G# - B - D# - (F#) - A#

C# minor 13 — "m13" 'should' contain all above notes but often omits 9th and 11th. The "m11" is also quite common and has 11th but no 13th.

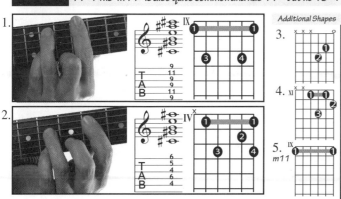

Additional Shapes

An unusual progression where "C#m13' in a fairly weak position begins the key change towards "A", which is never a convincing key centre.

VII	III	V	I
G#m9	C#m13	E7	A

C#-5   C# - E# - G

C# Flat 5 — Another tension chord that has a powerful need to resolve to the major chord.

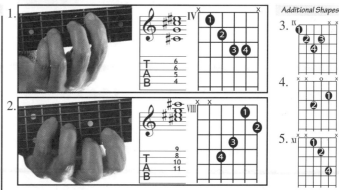

Additional Shapes

Not a standard 3 chord trick because the key, while beginning in "C#" modulates to "F#". The "C#-5 leads very finally to "F#6, the "6" confirms the finality.

I	IV	(IV) V	I
G#Δ7	C#7	C#-5	F#6

D — D - F♯ - A

D Major — The major triad is built using the 1st, 3rd and 5th notes from the major scale. It's the building block for all major & dominant chords.

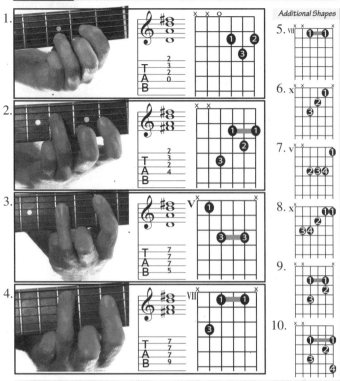

Additional Shapes

Classic chord progression with "D major" as the "I" chord. Ideal for acoustic in this key as there's opportunity to ring those open strings.

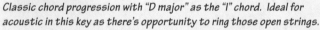

I	IV	VI	V
D	G	Bm	A

D△7(9) — D - F♯ - A - C♯ - (E)

D Major 7 (D Major 9) — Add the 7th note from the major scale to the major triad. The classic 'chill out' chord, very relaxed. Add 9th note for 'more'.

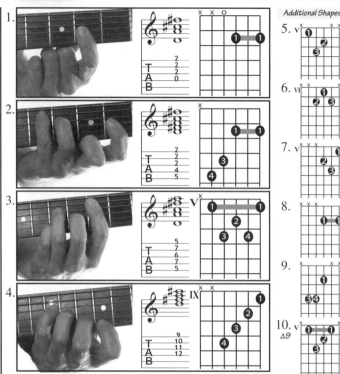

Additional Shapes

A common but interesting variation of the 3 chord trick. The interest is provided by the varying "D" chords where the melody is; "D"(D)-"C♯"(D△7)-"C"(D7)-"B"(D6).

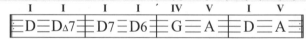

I	I	I	I	IV	V	I	V
D	D△7	D7	D6	G	A	D	A

D7 — D - F♯ - A - C

D dominant 7 — Add the 7th note from the minor scale to the MAJOR triad. Found mainly on the 5th note of the scale - powering back to the "I" chord.

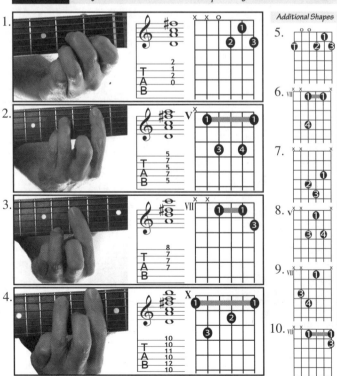

Additional Shapes

A major progression that's essentially "I"-"IV"-"V", the "Eb7" is a tension device that sees the "V7" raised 1 fret then returns to "D7" now even stronger, to set up "G".

I	IV	I	♭VI7	V
G	C7	G	Eb7	D7

D9 — D - F♯ - A - (C) - E

D9 and D add9 (D2) — The shapes of '9' and 'add 9' are similar but the sound of the full 9 chord is jazzier than 'add 9', as it includes the 7th.

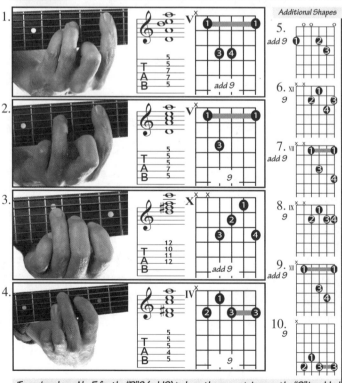

Additional Shapes

Try using shape No. 5 for the "D"2 (add9) to hear the open strings as the "9" is added more for its drifty effect than for progressing to the otherwise standard chords.

I	VI	I7	V
D2 (add9)	Bm7	D7	A7

Dm — D - F - A
D Minor
The minor triad is built using the 1st, 3rd and 5th notes from the minor scale. It's the building block for all minor chords.

Dm7 — D - F - A - C
D Minor 7
Add the 7th note from the minor scale to the minor triad. The character is milder, not so melancholic as the minor triad but is less positive.

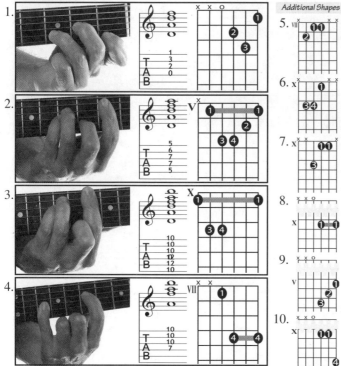
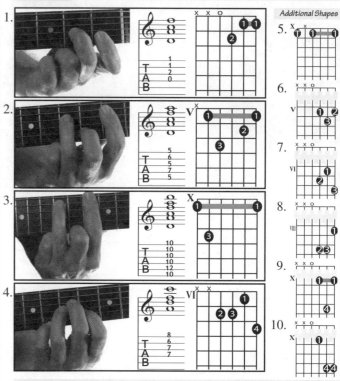

Additional Shapes

"Dm" leads out this classic minor chord progression and following the "A7", is the strongest you'll hear a minor chord.

I	VI	VII	I	V
Dm	B♭	C	Dm	A7

An obvious but not very popular progression. Is a bit lacking in character, the "m7" chords are always unobtrusive, even sleepy.

I	II	III	II
C△7	Dm7	Em7	Dm7

Dm9 — D - F - A - (C) - E
Dm9 and Dm add9
The shapes of 'm9' and 'm add 9' are similar but the sound of the 'm add9' chord is more 'mystic' than 'm9', as it omits the 7th.

D° diminished group — D - F - A♭ - (C(♭))
D°, D°7 & Dm7♭5
Diminished chords have similar fingerings and uses, the m7b5 adds a minor 7th and for °7 flatten the minor 7th another fret.

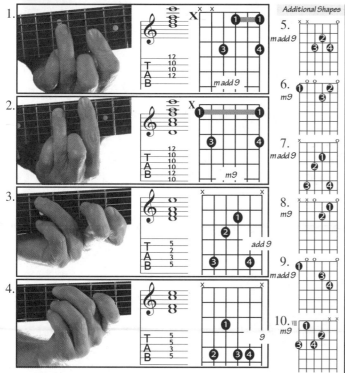
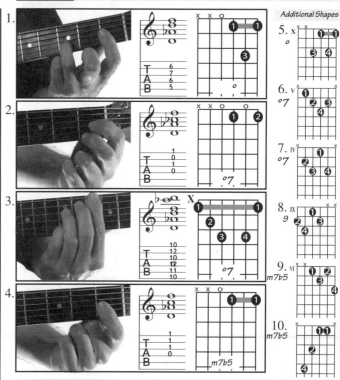

Additional Shapes

An unusual progression that changes key each chord. The 9's are added partly for their misty effect but also anticipate the following chord.

IV	V7	V	♭V7
Dm9	E9	Em7	E♭9

Classic chord progression that's made bluesy by adding 7's. The diminished chord is leading to "Eb7" but only teases as it repeats back to "Ab".

I	VI	IV	IV♯r
A♭7	Fm7	D♭7	D°

D

D6 — D - F♯ - A - B
D six
Add the sixth note of the major scale to the major triad. An instantly uplifting chord, some shapes sound like "m7", keep 6th high up in chord.

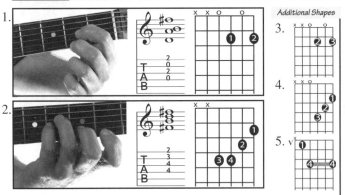

Additional Shapes
1. 2. 3. 4. 5.

Variation on a classic minor progression given quite a good makeover and disguise by adding "6"(B) to the "D" and "Δ7"(B) to the "C".

I	VII	VI	VII/VI	V
Em7	D6	CΔ7	D/C	Bm7

D6/9 — D - F♯ - A - B - E
D six nine
Add the 6th and 9th notes from major scale to major triad. Strange exotic blend of sounds can link unlikely chords together.

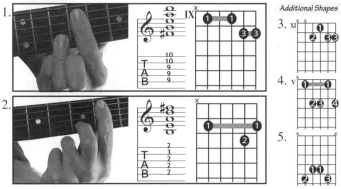

Additional Shapes
1. 2. 3. 4. 5.

Interesting treatment of regular "I"-"IV"-"V" chords. The chords sound very static and the "D6/9 gives an extra note to blend into both "G7" and "C6".

V	I	V	IV
D6/9	G7	D6/9	C6

Dsus4 — D - G - A
D suspended 4th
A major triad that has the 4th note of scale 'suspended' over the 3rd. A tense sound that is resolved by releasing 4th and hearing the 3rd.

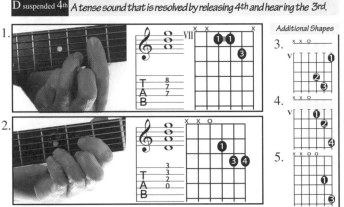

Additional Shapes
1. 2. 3. 4. 5.

Tension, release, tension, release is the trick here. Easiest way to achieve this; "sus", "major", "sus", "major". Listen to track 33 - similar.

I	I	V	V
Dsus	D	A7sus	A7

D5 — D - A - (D)
D5 (no 3rd) 'Power chord'
Take the 3rd out of any major/minor triad and you have a "5" chord. Most effective with loud electric playing, saves worrying about keys.

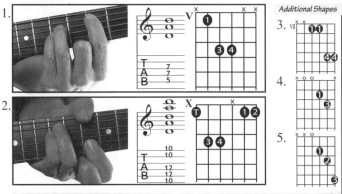

Additional Shapes
1. 2. 3. 4. 5.

Jumble up "I", "VI", "IV" and "V" chords a bit and then take out the 3rd's and you have an instant pop/rock song progression.

I	VI	I	IV	V	I
D5	B5	D5	G5	A5	D5

D13 — D - F♯ - A - C - E - (G) - B
D 13
13 chord 'should' contain all the above notes, in practice the 7th and 13th (=6th) are essential, the 9th richer, 11th unused. An exotic.

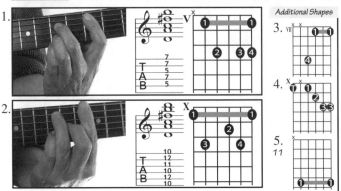

Additional Shapes
1. 2. 3. 4. 5.

Classic progression made slick and jazzy by adding generous helpings of chord extensions. Lots of common notes blend the chords into one another as they change.

I	VI	II	V
GΔ7	Em9	Am9	D13

D+ — D - F♯ - A♯
D augmented
Take a major triad and sharpen the 5th by 1 fret. Often used after the major, the sharp 5th progressing 1 fret at a time to next chord.

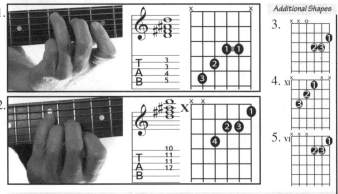

Additional Shapes
1. 2. 3. 4. 5.

Augmented in pivotal role. Stay on one root and move the "5th" up a semitone (fret) at a time. "A" (D), "A#" (D+), "B" (D6), "A#" (D+).

I	I	I	I
D	D+	D6	D+

Dm6 — D - F - A - B

D minor 6 Add the 6th from the major scale to a minor triad. The 6th is commonly added to the triad to give a 2nd note in common with next chord.

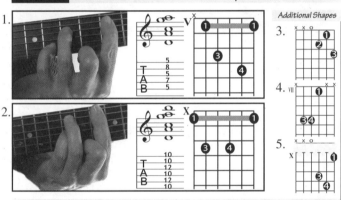

Additional Shapes

Quite a common progression where "II" & "VI" minor chords repeat and eventually settle on "I". The "6" (B) is added as it leads to the "C" in both "Am7" & "C".

II	VI	II	I
Dm6	Am7	Dm6	C

Dm Δ7 — D - F - A - C#

D minor major 7 Add the 7th from the major scale to a minor triad. Rarely used on its own. Usually follows either "m7","m" or "m6". Similar to augmented.

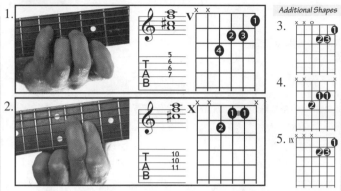

Additional Shapes

Seemingly routine 3 chord trick transformed by thinking about melody. Find shapes that enable you to hear; "D" (D), "C#" (DΔ7), "C" (D7), "B" (D6), "Bb" (Gm6), "A" (A7).

I	I	I	I	IV	V
Dm	DmΔ7	Dm7	Dm6	Gm6	A7

D7sus4 — D - G - A - C

D seven suspended 4th With a flat (minor) 7th AND a suspended 4th this chord is over-loaded with tension. Sometimes used in place of the "11" chord.

Additional Shapes

3 chord trick variation loaded to excess on the "V" chord using "7sus4" to "major". The "I" and "IV" chords provide the release points.

I	V	V	IV	V	V
G	D7sus	D	C	D7sus	D

D7#9 — D - F# - A - C - E# (=F)

D7 sharp 9 Wickedly tense, a regular 7 chord with a sharp 9th (equal to sticking a minor 3rd on top). Usually on either 5th or 1st notes of the scale.

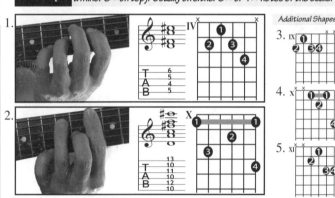

Additional Shapes

Not very common as chords go but demonstrates how you can get away with dramatic change if the notes run logically. "D" & "F" from the "7#9" move to "E".

V	VI7	V	V
D7#9	E9	D7#9	G

Dm13 — D - F - A - C - E - (G) - B

D minor 13 "m13" 'should' contain all above notes but often omits 9th and 11th. The "m11" is also quite common and has 11th but no 13th.

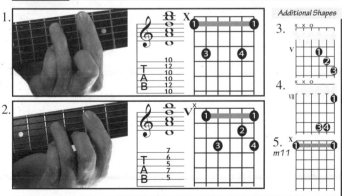

Additional Shapes

An unusual minor progression that's tricky to find the right shapes and movement. Try having "B", "B", "C" and "D" as your highest notes.

IV	V7	III	IV
Dm13	E7	Cm7	Dm7

D-5 — D - F# - Ab

D flat 5 Another tension chord that has a powerful need to resolve to the major chord.

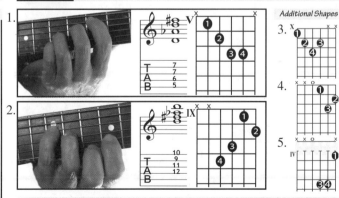

Additional Shapes

An interesting progression that needs to be played in such a way that you clearly hear the melody; "A" (D), "Ab" (D-5), "G" (G), "Bb" (Gm).

V	V	I	I
D	D-5	G	Gm

E♭ — E♭ - G - B♭

E♭ Major — The major triad is built using the 1st, 3rd and 5th notes from the major scale. It's the building block for all major & dominant chords.

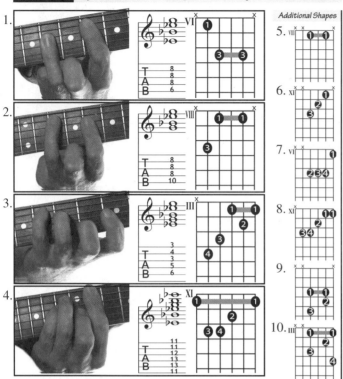

A typical rock and guitar approach to chord progressions is a mixture of two keys; "B♭" & "C". "E♭" is 'wrong' to be major for "C" but "C" is actually the new key. So what, it rocks!

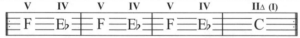

V	IV	V	IV	V	IV	II△ (I)
F	E♭	F	E♭	F	E♭	C

E♭△7(9) — E♭ - G - B♭ - D

E♭ Major 7 / E♭ Major 9 — Add the 7th note from the major scale to the major triad. The classic 'chill out' chord, very relaxed. Add 9th note for 'more'.

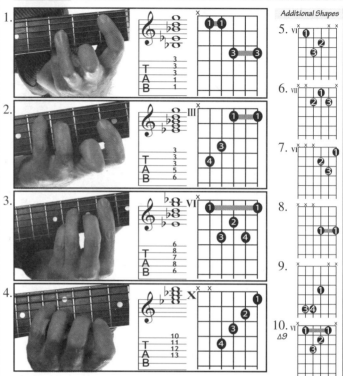

Really cool chord progression that is not as used as it could be. The "E♭△7" on "IV" sounds very like a "I" chord - very stable.

IV	III	II	V
E♭△7	Dm7	Cm7	F7

E♭7 — E♭ - G - B♭ - D♭

E♭ dominant 7 — Add the 7th note from the minor scale to the MAJOR triad. Found mainly on the 5th note of the scale - powering back to the "I" chord.

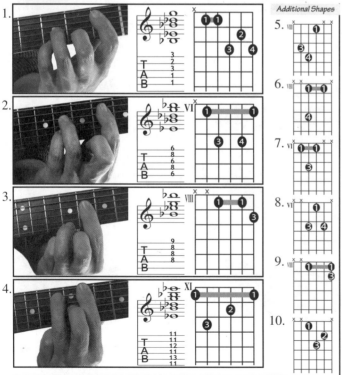

Interesting chord progression that could go on forever, as what starts out as a "II"-"V"-"I" becomes cyclic as the "I" becomes "II" of the next key and so on.

II	V	II	V	II	V
Dm7	G7	Cm7	F7	B♭m7	E♭7

E♭9 — E♭ - G - B♭ - (D♭) - F

E♭ 9 / E♭ add9 (E♭2) — The shapes of '9' and 'add 9' are similar but the sound of the full 9 chord is jazzier than 'add 9 ', as it includes the 7th.

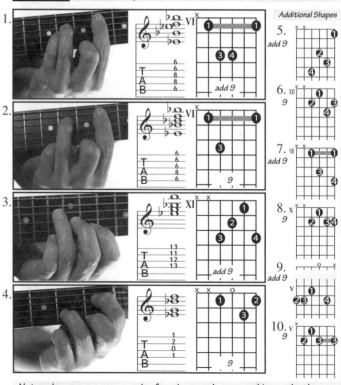

Not such a common progression for minor, made more ambiguous by the "E♭9". The real trick to playing is to keep B♭ as the highest note on all chords.

I7	IV	III	V
E♭9	A♭m add9	G♭△7	B♭7

E♭m — E♭ Minor — E♭ - G♭ - B♭

The minor triad is built using the 1st, 3rd and 5th notes from the minor scale. It's the building block for all minor chords.

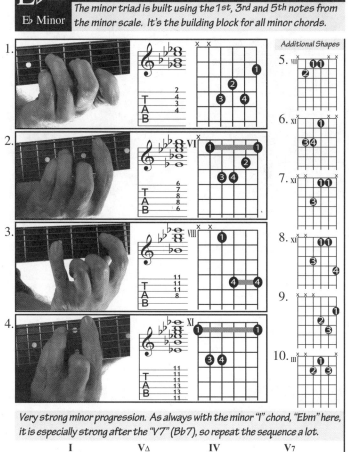

Additional Shapes
5. VIII
6. XI
7. XI
8. XI
9.
10. III

Very strong minor progression. As always with the minor "I" chord, "Ebm" here, it is especially strong after the "V7" (Bb7), so repeat the sequence a lot.

I	VΔ	IV	V7
E♭m	B♭	A♭m	B♭7

E♭m7 — E♭ Minor 7 — E♭ - G♭ - B♭ - D♭

Add the 7th note from the minor scale to the minor triad. The character is milder, not so melancholic as the minor triad but is less positive.

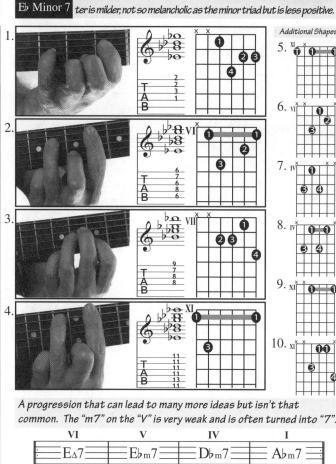

Additional Shapes
5. XI
6. VI
7. IV
8. IV
9. XI
10. XI

A progression that can lead to many more ideas but isn't that common. The "m7" on the "V" is very weak and is often turned into "7".

VI	V	IV	I
EΔ7	E♭m7	D♭m7	A♭m7

E♭m9 — E♭m9 and E♭m add9 — E♭ - G♭ - B♭ - (D♭) - F

The shapes of 'm9' and 'm add9' are similar but the sound of the 'm add9' chord is more 'mystic' than 'm9', as it omits the 7th.

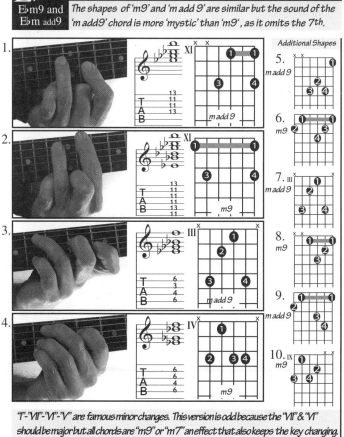

Additional Shapes
5. m add 9
6. m9
7. III m add 9
8. m9
9. m add 9
10. IX m9

"I"-"VII"-"VI"-"V" are famous minor changes. This version is odd because the "VII" & "VI" should be major but all chords are "m9" or "m7" an effect that also keeps the key changing.

Im	Im	VII		VI		V
E♭m9	E♭m7	D♭m9	D♭m7	Bm9	Bm7	B♭7

E♭° diminished group — E♭°, E♭°7, E♭m7b5 — E♭ - G♭ - B♭♭ - (D♭/D♭♭)

Diminished chords have similar fingerings and uses, the m7b5 adds a minor 7th and for °7 flatten the minor 7th another fret.

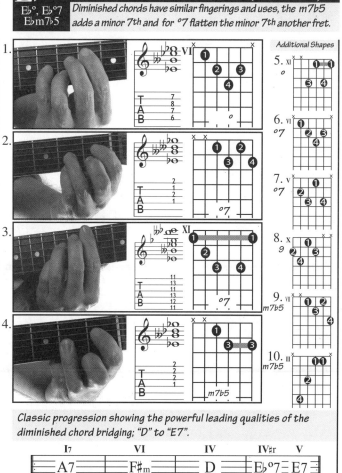

Additional Shapes
5. XI °
6. VI °7
7. V °7
8. X 9
9. VII m7b5
10. II m7b5

Classic progression showing the powerful leading qualities of the diminished chord bridging; "D" to "E7".

I7	VI	IV	IV#r	V
A7	F♯m	D	E♭°7	E7

E♭/D♯

E♭6 — E♭ - G - B♭ - C

E♭ Major — Add the sixth note of the major scale to the major triad. An instantly uplifting chord, some shapes sound like "m7", keep 6th high up in chord.

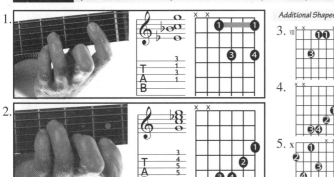

Additional Shapes

The key centre is ambiguous - is it "Eb" or "F". The addition of the "6" is useful for linking into Fm but weakens the chord sound until "Bb7" restores key to "F".

VII	I	VI	IV₇
E♭6	Fm	D♭	B♭7

E♭6/9 — E♭ - G - B♭ - C - F

E♭ six nine — Add the 6th and 9th notes from major scale to major triad. Strange exotic blend of sounds can link unlikely chords together.

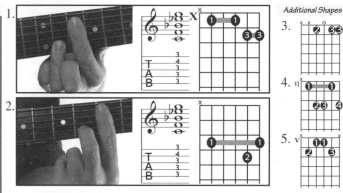

Additional Shapes

Unusual progression with each chord holding notes form the previous chord to make the changes slick - without the extensions progression is very jumbled.

I	IV	♭VII	VI
E♭6/9	A♭9	D♭m9	Cm7♭5

E♭sus4 — E♭ - A♭ - B♭

E♭ suspended 4th — A major triad that has the 4th note of scale 'suspended' over the 3rd. A tense sound that is resolved by releasing 4th and hearing the 3rd.

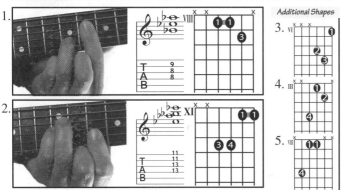

Additional Shapes

Really interesting use of the "sus" chord, here on the "I" chord, the suspended 4th is the link to an unusual but effective "Δ7" chord on the 'b II', great tension.

I	♭II	V	I
E♭sus	EΔ7	B♭7	E♭

E♭5 — E♭ - B♭ - (E♭)

E♭5 (no 3rd) 'Power chord' — Take the 3rd out of any major/minor triad and you have a "5" chord. Most effective with loud electric playing, saves worrying about keys.

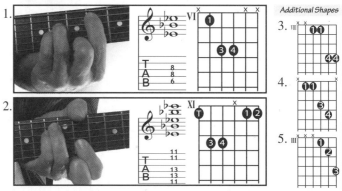

Additional Shapes

This classic progression has spawned so many songs, taking out the 3rd's gives it new and instantly rocky life.

I	VI	IV	V
A♭5	F5	D♭5	E♭5

E♭13 — E♭ - G - B♭ - D♭ - F - (A♭) - C

E♭ 13 — 13 chord 'should' contain all the above notes, in practice the 7th and 13th (=6th) are essential, the 9th richer, 11th unused. An exotic.

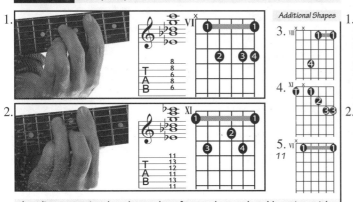

Additional Shapes

A cyclic progression that changes key after two bars and would continue without the intervention of the "Bbm" which crudely takes you back to "Eb13".

V	I	V	I	II
E♭13	A♭7	D♭13	G♭7	B♭m

E♭+ — E♭ - G - B

E♭ augmented — Take a major triad and sharpen the 5th by 1 fret. Often used after the major, the sharp 5th progressing 1 fret at a time to next chord.

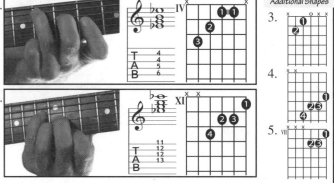

Additional Shapes

Chords that make their own melody, here the augmented provides the link from "Eb" to "Ab" but progression melody; "Bb"(Eb)-"B"(Eb+)-"C"(Ab)-"Cb(B)" (Abm).

I	I	IV	IVm
E♭	E♭+	A♭	A♭m

32

Ebm6   Eb - Gb - Bb - C

Eb Minor six

Add the 6th from the major scale to a minor triad. The 6th is commonly added to the triad to give a 2nd note in common with next chord.

Additional Shapes

Well worn progression "II"-"V" repeating before settling onto the "I" chord. The "6" added to Ebm6 means there's only one note to change for Ab7 (Bb-Ab) - slick.

II	V	II	I
Ebm6	Ab7	Ebm6	Db6

Ebm△7   Eb - Gb - Bb - D

Eb minor major seven

Add the 7th from the major scale to a minor triad. Rarely used on its own. Usually follows either "m7","m" or "m6". Similar to augmented.

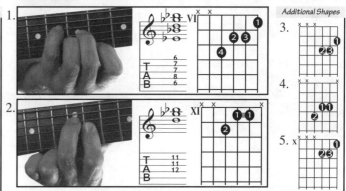

Additional Shapes

The "m△7" chord usually acts as a passing chord, the melody line created here is "Eb" (Ebm), "D" (Ebm△7), "C" (Db△7), "Bb" (Bb7).

I	I	VII	V	I	I	VII	V
Ebm	Ebm△7	Db△7	Bbm	Ebm	Ebm△7	Db△7	Bb7

Eb7sus4   Eb - Ab - Bb - Db

Eb seven suspended 4th

With a flat (minor) 7th AND a suspended 4th this chord is over-loaded with tension. Sometimes used in place of the "11" chord.

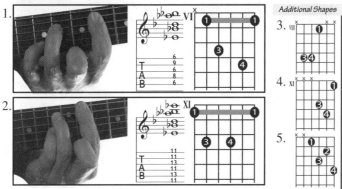

Additional Shapes

What could have been yet another "V"-"IV"-"I" progression is transformed by using the suspended 4 to anchor a raised "V7" for drama and tension.

V	bVI7	IV	I
Eb7sus	E7	Db	Ab

Eb7#9   Eb - G - Bb - Db - F#

Eb seven sharp nine

Wickedly tense, a regular 7 chord with a sharp 9th (equal to sticking a minor 3rd on top). Usually on either 5th or 1st notes of the scale.

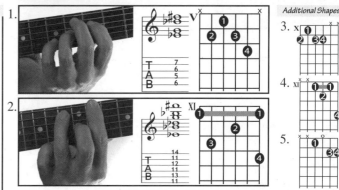

Additional Shapes

Great to hear the "7#9" chord as part of a minor progression, the slight key change on "E7" gets the ball rolling and the "D#7#9" really kicks.

I	VI	I	V
G#m	E7	G#m	D#7#9

Ebm13   Eb - Gb - Bb - Db - F - (Ab) - C

Eb minor 13

"m13" 'should' contain all above notes but often omits 9th and 11th. The "m11" is also quite common and has 11th but no 13th.

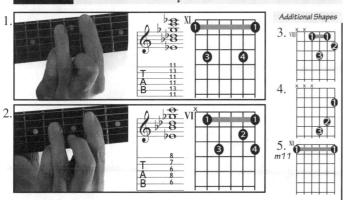

Additional Shapes

A really sumptuous progression that can be played fast and funky or slow and ambient. "Bbm9" to "Ebm13" is just so smooth.

I	IV	bVII	V
Bbm9	Ebm13	Abm9	F7

Eb-5   Eb - G - Bbb (=A)

Eb flat 5

Another tension chord that has a powerful need to resolve to the major chord.

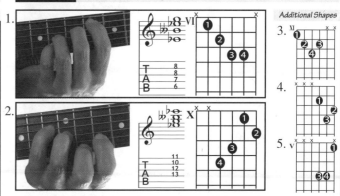

Additional Shapes

A simple 2 chord progression that attracts attention by creating an intentional discord on the final 2 Eb-5's. No other function - just crude and dramatic.

I	IV	I	I
Eb	Ab	Eb-5	Eb-5

E

E — E Major — E - G# - B

The major triad is built using the 1st, 3rd and 5th notes from the major scale. It's the building block for all major & dominant chords.

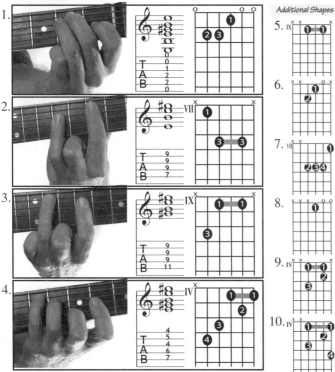

Additional Shapes

It's one of those famous progressions that could be a thousand pop and rock songs. Easy to play and create melody to. Go have a hit.

I	IV	VI	V
E	A	C#m	B

EΔ7(9) — E Major 7 (E Major 9) — E - G# - B - D# - (F#)

Add the 7th note from the major scale to the major triad. The classic 'chill out' chord, very relaxed. Add 9th note for 'more'.

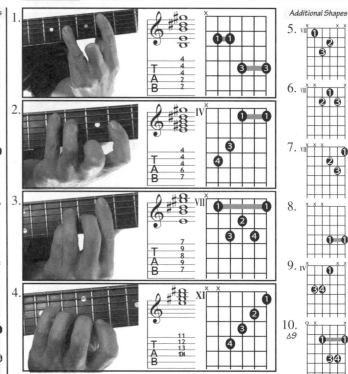

Additional Shapes

A great major 7 progression. The dramatic key change from "EΔ7" to "CΔ7" where you expect the predictable "BΔ7" to come in is fantastic.

IV	#IΔ7	IV	V (no root)
EΔ7	CΔ7	EΔ7	Bb°

E7 — E dominant 7 — E - G# - B - D

Add the 7th note from the minor scale to the MAJOR triad. Found mainly on the 5th note of the scale - powering back to the "I" chord.

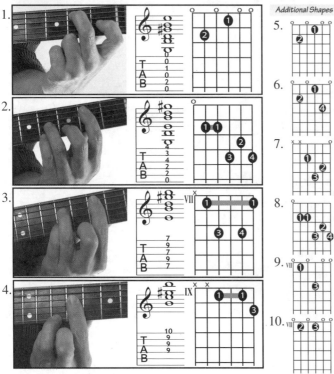

Additional Shapes

They don't come much more predictable than this - all dominant 7 chords means a new key each chord - blues style. Predictable but fun.

I	IV	I	V
E7	A7	E7	B7

E9 — E9 and E add9 (E2) — E - G# - B - (D) - F#

The shapes of '9' and 'add 9' are similar but the sound of the full 9 chord is jazzier than 'add 9', as it includes the 7th.

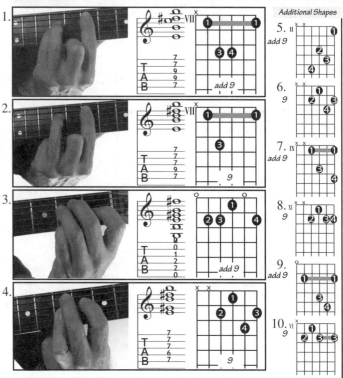

Additional Shapes

The change from "E add9" (or E2) to "G#7" is stunning. It's always a great effect to hear the lll chord change the key by becoming "7", but after E2 - amazing.

I	III7 (V)	(I)VI	bVII
E add9	G#7	C#m7	D-5

34

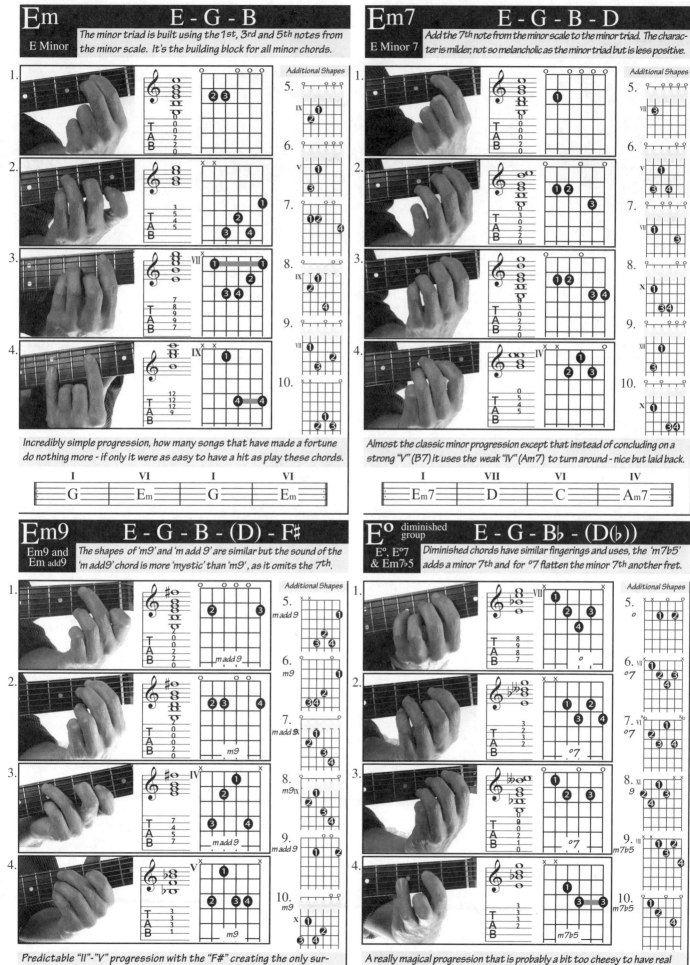

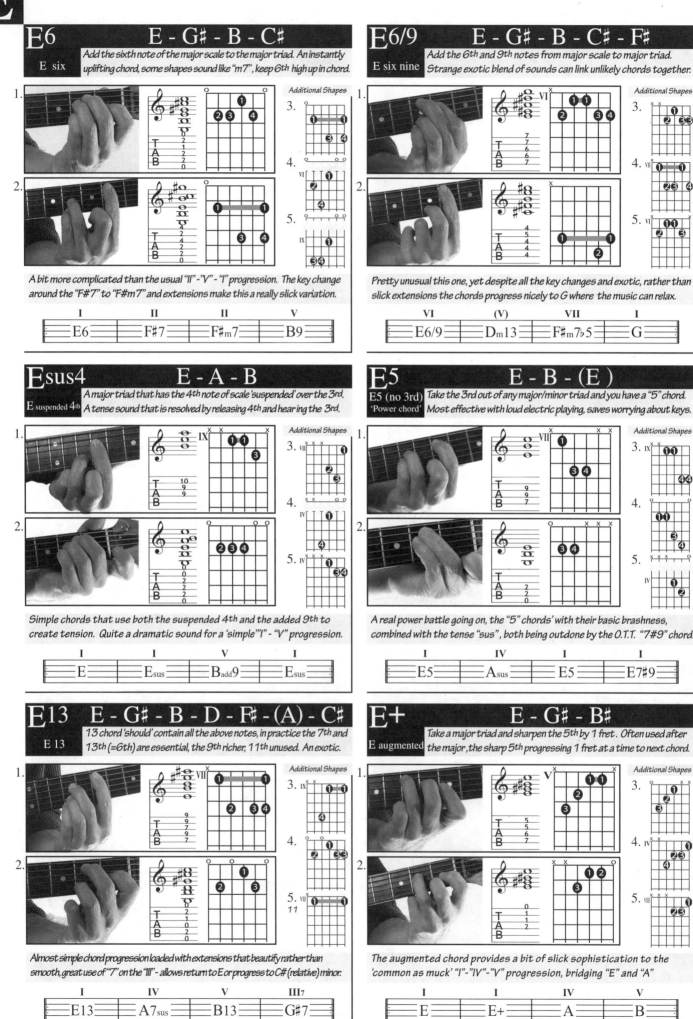

E6 — E - G♯ - B - C♯

E six

Add the sixth note of the major scale to the major triad. An instantly uplifting chord, some shapes sound like "m7", keep 6th high up in chord.

Additional Shapes 3. 4. 5.

A bit more complicated than the usual "II"-"V"-"I" progression. The key change around the "F#7" to "F#m7" and extensions make this a really slick variation.

I	II	II	V
E6	F#7	F#m7	B9

E6/9 — E - G♯ - B - C♯ - F♯

E six nine

Add the 6th and 9th notes from major scale to major triad. Strange exotic blend of sounds can link unlikely chords together.

Additional Shapes 3. 4. 5.

Pretty unusual this one, yet despite all the key changes and exotic, rather than slick extensions the chords progress nicely to G where the music can relax.

VI	(V)	VII	I
E6/9	Dm13	F#m7♭5	G

Esus4 — E - A - B

E suspended 4th

A major triad that has the 4th note of scale 'suspended' over the 3rd. A tense sound that is resolved by releasing 4th and hearing the 3rd.

Additional Shapes 3. 4. 5.

Simple chords that use both the suspended 4th and the added 9th to create tension. Quite a dramatic sound for a 'simple' "I" - "V" progression.

I	I	V	I
E	Esus	Badd9	Esus

E5 — E - B - (E)

E5 (no 3rd) 'Power chord'

Take the 3rd out of any major/minor triad and you have a "5" chord. Most effective with loud electric playing, saves worrying about keys.

Additional Shapes 3. 4. 5.

A real power battle going on, the "5" chords' with their basic brashness, combined with the tense "sus", both being outdone by the O.T.T. "7#9" chord.

I	IV	I	I
E5	Asus	E5	E7#9

E13 — E - G♯ - B - D - F♯ - (A) - C♯

E 13

13 chord 'should' contain all the above notes, in practice the 7th and 13th (=6th) are essential, the 9th richer, 11th unused. An exotic.

Additional Shapes 3. 4. 5.

Almost simple chord progression loaded with extensions that beautify rather than smooth, great use of "7" on the "III" - allows return to E or progress to C# (relative) minor.

I	IV	V	III7
E13	A7sus	B13	G#7

E+ — E - G♯ - B♯

E augmented

Take a major triad and sharpen the 5th by 1 fret. Often used after the major, the sharp 5th progressing 1 fret at a time to next chord.

Additional Shapes 3. 4. 5.

The augmented chord provides a bit of slick sophistication to the 'common as muck' "I"-"IV"-"V" progression, bridging "E" and "A"

I	I	IV	V
E	E+	A	B

Em6 — E - G - B - C#
E minor 6

Add the 6th from the major scale to a minor triad. The 6th is commonly added to the triad to give a 2nd note in common with next chord.

1.
2.

Additional Shapes
3. v
4.
5. x

What begins life as a regular (if not over common) "VI"-"I"-"IV"-"V" progression is deliberately distorted with key change by adding "6" to "Em" and the "7" to G.

VI	I7	IV	V
Em6	G7	C△7	D7

Em△7 — E - G - B - D#
E minor major 7

Add the 7th from the major scale to a minor triad. Rarely used on its own. Usually follows either "m7", "m" or "m6". Similar to augmented.

1. VII
2.

Additional Shapes
3.
4.
5. XI

An interesting blend of chord sound doing the same job a different way. Both pairs of chords play "E"-"D#" as a melody - nice effect.

I	I	V	V
Em	Em△7	B7sus	B7

E7sus4 — E - A - B - D
E seven suspended 4th

With a flat (minor) 7th AND a suspended 4th this chord is overloaded with tension. Sometimes used in place of the "11" chord.

1. VII
2.

Additional Shapes
3.
4. IX
5. IV

Fairly gentle sound for "7 sus4". Probably because it comes out of "m7" not "7" and because "Bm7" retains the A (4th) for its 7th.

I	I	V	V
Em7	E7sus	Bm7	Bm7

E7#9 — E - G# - B - D - F## (=G)
E7 sharp 9

Wickedly tense, a regular 7 chord with a sharp 9th (equal to sticking a minor 3rd on top). Usually on either 5th or 1st notes of the scale.

1. VI
2.

Additional Shapes
3. XI
4.
5.

The "7#9" always sounds good coming out of a "7" chord raised 1 fret up from "V". Adding the "9" is an obvious extension, sounds great but really tames the "7#9".

#V(VI)	V	I	I
F9	E7#9	A7	A7

Em13 E - G - B - D - F# - (A) - C#
E minor 13

"m13" should' contain all above notes but often omits 9th and 11th. The "m11" is also quite common and has 11th but no 13th.

1.
2. VII

Additional Shapes
3.
4. III
5. m11

The "m13" is really excess baggage structurally, but has an exotic character that lifts the progression above average.

IV	I	VI	V
Em13	Bm7	G	F#7

E-5 — E - G# - Bb
E flat 5

Another tension chord that has a powerful need to resolve to the major chord.

1. VII
2. XI

Additional Shapes
3.
4.
5. VI

Simple progression that uses "E-5" to link from "E" to "A", a kind of link that can be played for a while for tension and is mimicked by the "A" changing to "Am".

I	I	IV	IVm
E	E-5	A	Am

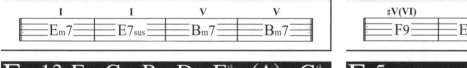
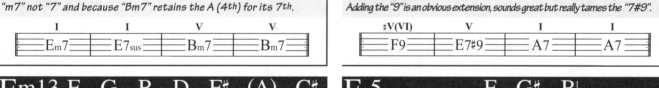
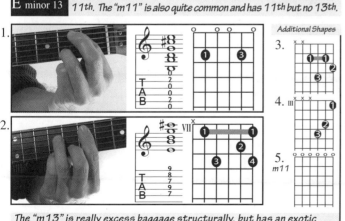

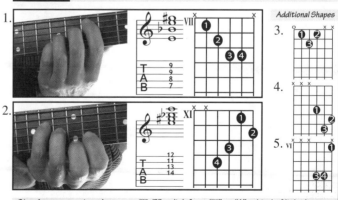

F

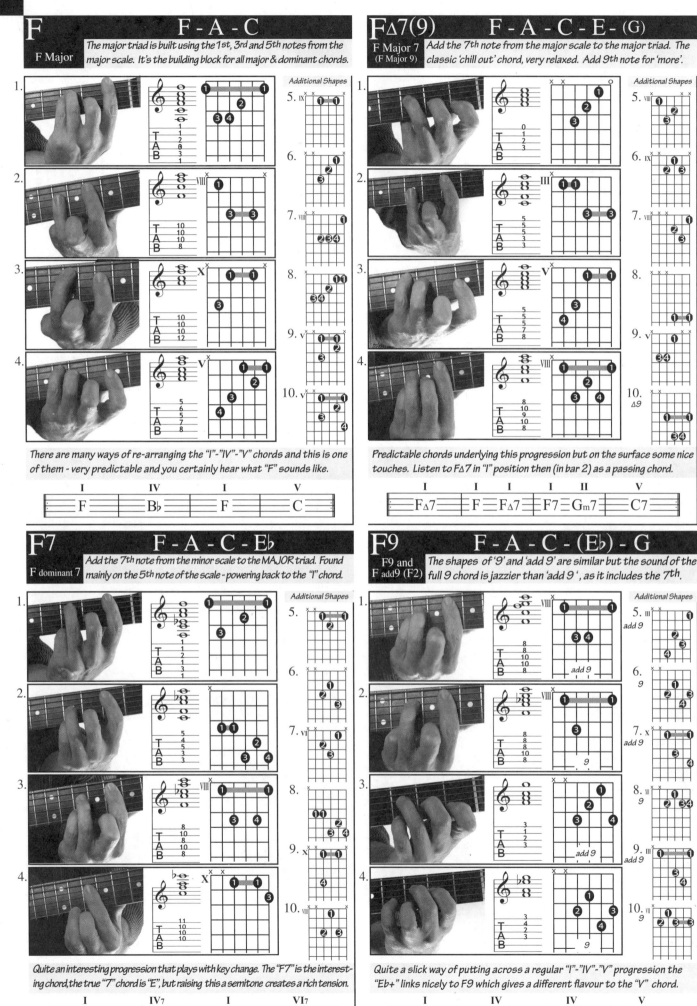

F — **F - A - C**
F Major

The major triad is built using the 1st, 3rd and 5th notes from the major scale. It's the building block for all major & dominant chords.

Additional Shapes

There are many ways of re-arranging the "I"-"IV"-"V" chords and this is one of them - very predictable and you certainly hear what "F" sounds like.

I	IV	I	V
F	B♭	F	C

F∆7(9) — **F - A - C - E - (G)**
F Major 7 (F Major 9)

Add the 7th note from the major scale to the major triad. The classic 'chill out' chord, very relaxed. Add 9th note for 'more'.

Additional Shapes

Predictable chords underlying this progression but on the surface some nice touches. Listen to F∆7 in "I" position then (in bar 2) as a passing chord.

I	I	I	I	II	V
F∆7	F	F∆7	F7	Gm7	C7

F7 — **F - A - C - E♭**
F dominant 7

Add the 7th note from the minor scale to the MAJOR triad. Found mainly on the 5th note of the scale - powering back to the "I" chord.

Additional Shapes

Quite an interesting progression that plays with key change. The "F7" is the interesting chord, the true "7" chord is "E", but raising this a semitone creates a rich tension.

I	IV7	I	VI7
Am	D7	Am	F7

F9 — **F - A - C - (E♭) - G**
F9 and F add9 (F2)

The shapes of '9' and 'add 9' are similar but the sound of the full 9 chord is jazzier than 'add 9 ', as it includes the 7th.

Additional Shapes

Quite a slick way of putting across a regular "I"-"IV"-"V" progression the "Eb+" links nicely to F9 which gives a different flavour to the "V" chord.

I	IV	IV	V
B♭	E♭	E♭+	F9

38

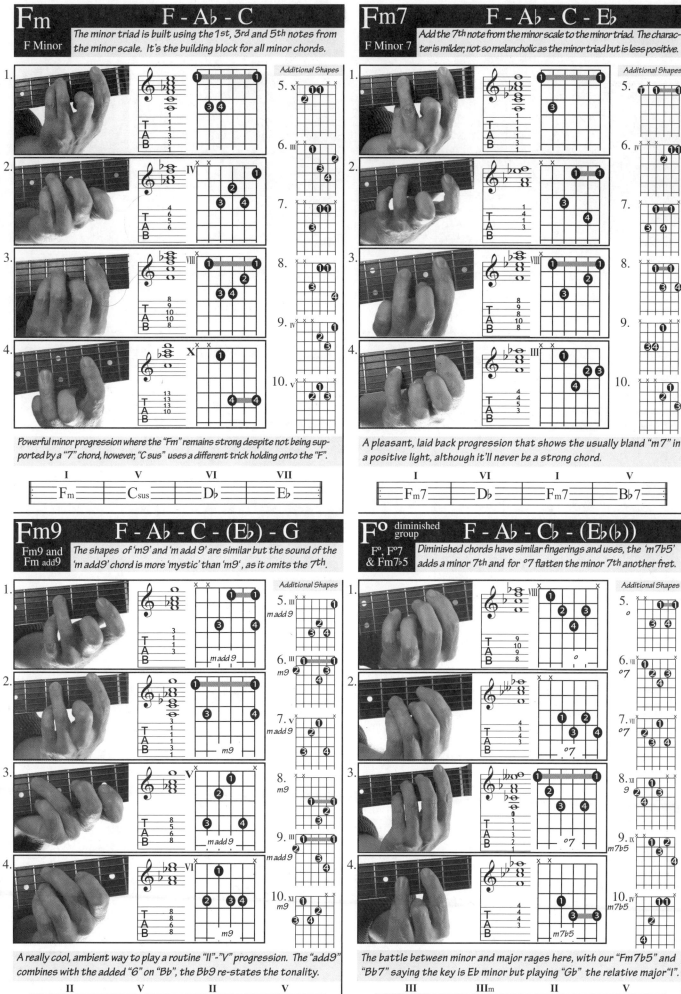

F

F6   F - A - C - D
F six   Add the sixth note of the major scale to the major triad. An instantly uplifting chord, some shapes sound like "m7", keep 6th high up in chord.

F6/9   F - A - C - D - G
F six nine   Add the 6th and 9th notes from major scale to major triad. Strange exotic blend of sounds can link unlikely chords together.

Fsus4   F - Bb - C
F suspended 4th   A major triad that has the 4th note of scale 'suspended' over the 3rd. A tense sound that is resolved by releasing 4th and hearing the 3rd.

F5   F - C - (F)
F5 (no 3rd)   Take the 3rd out of any major/minor triad and you have a "5" chord.
'Power chord'   Most effective with loud electric playing, saves worrying about keys.

F13   F - A - C - Eb - G - (Bb) - D
F 13   13 chord 'should' contain all the above notes, in practice the 7th and 13th (=6th) are essential, the 9th richer, 11th unused. An exotic.

F+   F - A - C#
F augmented   Take a major triad and sharpen the 5th by 1 fret. Often used after the major, the sharp 5th progressing 1 fret at a time to next chord.

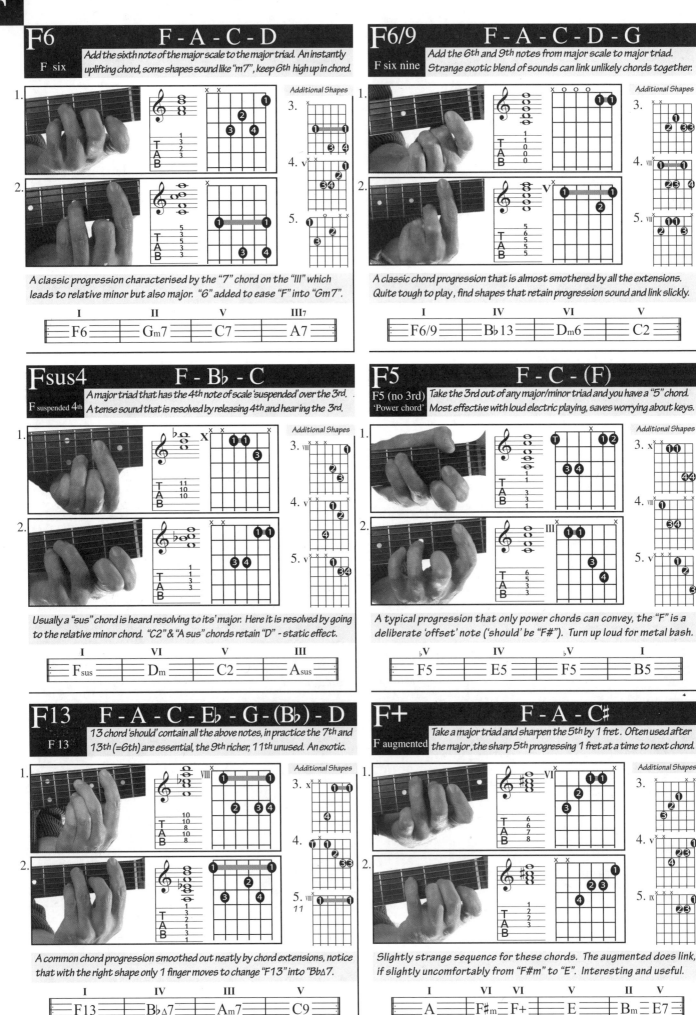

Additional Shapes

A classic progression characterised by the "7" chord on the "III" which leads to relative minor but also major. "6" added to ease "F" into "Gm7".

I	II	V	III₇
F6	Gm7	C7	A7

A classic chord progression that is almost smothered by all the extensions. Quite tough to play, find shapes that retain progression sound and link slickly.

I	IV	VI	V
F6/9	Bb13	Dm6	C2

Usually a "sus" chord is heard resolving to its' major. Here it is resolved by going to the relative minor chord. "C2" & "A sus" chords retain "D" - static effect.

I	VI	V	III
Fsus	Dm	C2	Asus

A typical progression that only power chords can convey, the "F" is a deliberate 'offset' note ('should' be "F#"). Turn up loud for metal bash.

bV	IV	bV	I
F5	E5	F5	B5

A common chord progression smoothed out neatly by chord extensions, notice that with the right shape only 1 finger moves to change "F13" into "Bb△7".

I	IV	III	V
F13	Bb△7	Am7	C9

Slightly strange sequence for these chords. The augmented does link, if slightly uncomfortably from "F#m" to "E". Interesting and useful.

I	VI	VI	V	II	V
A	F#m	F+	E	Bm	E7

40

Fm6   F - A♭ - C - D

F minor 6 — Add the 6th from the major scale to a minor triad. The 6th is commonly added to the triad to give a 2nd note in common with next chord.

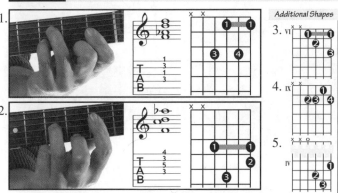

Additional Shapes

1.
2.
3. vi
4. ix
5. iv

A "II"-"V"-"I" progression with a twist, the "Gm7b5" tries to take it into F minor. "6" added to Fm to give 2 common notes with "Bb7".

II	V	I	III (II)
Fm6	B♭7	E♭△7	Gm7♭5

Fm △7   F - A♭ - C - E

F minor major 7 — Add the 7th from the major scale to a minor triad. Rarely used on its own. Usually follows either "m7", "m" or "m6". Similar to augmented.

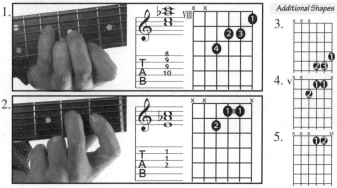

Additional Shapes

1.
2.
3.
4. v
5.

An really strong minor progression that changes key on the "Bb" enough to keep you guessing. The "m△7" links slickly from "Fm" to "Ab".

I	I	III	IV	VI	V
Fm	Fm△7	A♭	B♭	D♭	C7

F7sus4   F - B♭ - C - E♭

F seven suspended 4th — With a flat (minor) 7th AND a suspended 4th this chord is overloaded with tension. Sometimes used in place of the "11" chord.

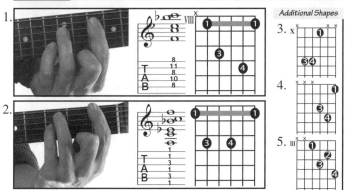

Additional Shapes

1.
2.
3. x
4.
5. iii

The classic "II"-"V"-"I" progression given the "7 sus4" treatment on the "V" chord which gives interest and power to an otherwise tame progression.

II	V	V	I
Cm7	F7sus	F	B♭

F7#9   F - A - C - E♭ - G#

F7 sharp 9 — Wickedly tense, a regular 7 chord with a sharp 9th (equal to sticking a minor 3rd on top). Usually on either 5th or 1st notes of the scale.

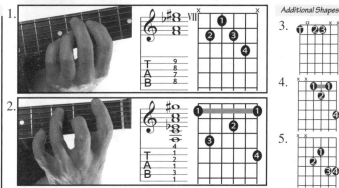

Additional Shapes

1.
2.
3.
4.
5.

Normally the "7#9" occurs on the "V" chord. Here it is used as a highly charged "I" chord that could go on building tension for many bars, released by "IV" & "V".

I	I	IV	V
F7#9	F7#9	B♭	C

Fm13   F - A♭ - C - E♭ - G - (B♭) - D

F minor 13 — "m13" 'should' contain all above notes but often omits 9th and 11th. The "m11" is also quite common and has 11th but no 13th.

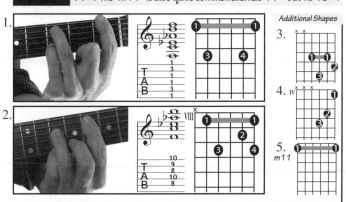

Additional Shapes

1.
2.
3.
4. iv
5. m11

Strong minor progression smoothed out with extensions. The point of adding so many notes to "Fm" is that "Cm" is contained within it as are 2 notes from "Bb".

I	IV	VII	V
Cm7	Fm13	B♭	G7

F-5   F - A - C♭

F flat 5 — Another tension chord that has a powerful need to resolve to the major chord.

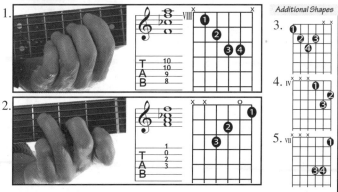

Additional Shapes

1.
2.
3.
4. iv
5. vii

"IV"-"II"-"I" is a slightly uncomfortable progression. However, flattening the 5th on "F" and adding "6" to Dm adds a "B" that sings sweetly through all 4 chords.

IV	II	I	I
F-5	Dm6	C△7	C△7

F# — F# - A# - C#

F# Major — The major triad is built using the 1st, 3rd and 5th notes from the major scale. It's the building block for all major & dominant chords.

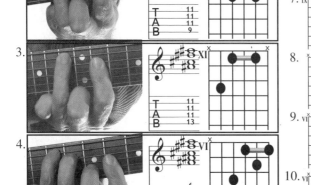

Additional Shapes

Routine progression, although "I"-"III"-"VI" isn't that common. "Gb (F#)" is strong in the "I" position, interesting that only the root of "V" (in "IV" chord) is needed to repeat.

I	III	VI	IV	IV/V
Gb	Bbm	Ebm	Cb	Cb/Db

F#∆7(9) — F# - A# - C#- E#

F# Major 7 (F# Major 9) — Add the 7th note from the major scale to the major triad. The classic 'chill out' chord, very relaxed. Add 9th note for 'more'.

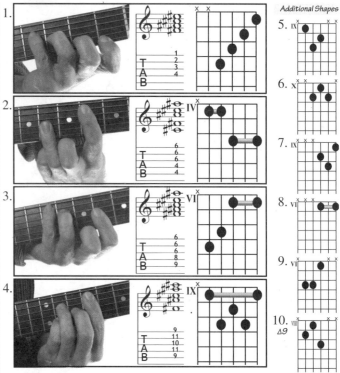

Additional Shapes

Simple chords made to sound really relaxed by added the "∆7" to the "F#" ("I") chord, padded out with first major, then "7" on the "V" chord.

I	VI	V	V
F#∆7	D#m	C#	C#7

F#7 — F# - A# - C#- E

F# Dominant 7 — Add the 7th note from the minor scale to the MAJOR triad. Found mainly on the 5th note of the scale - powering back to the "I" chord.

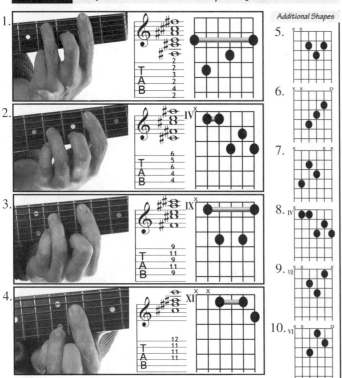

Additional Shapes

At first glance the classic "I"-"VI"-"II"-"V" progression in "A" however, "F#7" (you expect F#m) changes this so that "E" is the real key centre.

IV	II7 (V)	V (I)	I
A	F#7	B7	E

F#9 — F# - A# - C# - (E) - C#

F# 9 and F# add 9 (F#2) — The shapes of '9' and 'add 9' are similar but the sound of the full 9 chord is jazzier than 'add 9', as it includes the 7th.

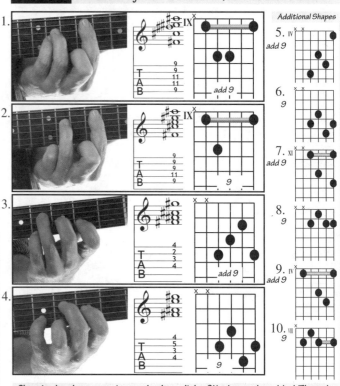

Additional Shapes

Classic chord progression made ultra slick - OK, cheesy, by added 7's and 9's. Adding "9" (&"7") to "F#" allows "F#" to retain 2 notes from "C#m7".

II	V	I	VI
C#m7	F#9	B∆7	G#m7

F#m — F# - A - C#

F# Minor — The minor triad is built using the 1st, 3rd and 5th notes from the minor scale. It's the building block for all minor chords.

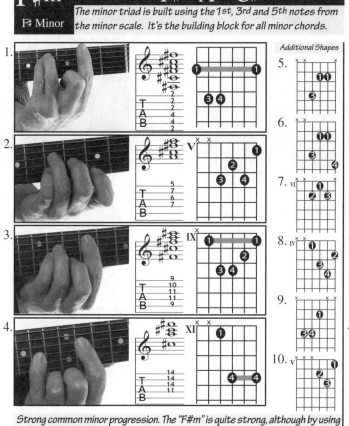

Additional Shapes

Strong common minor progression. The "F#m" is quite strong, although by using "C#2" on turn-around (repeat) the effect is similar but weaker than using "C#7".

I	IV	VII	V
F#m	Bm	E	C#2

F#m7 — F# - A - C# - E

F# minor 7 — Add the 7th note from the minor scale to the minor triad. The character is milder, not so melancholic as the minor triad but is less positive.

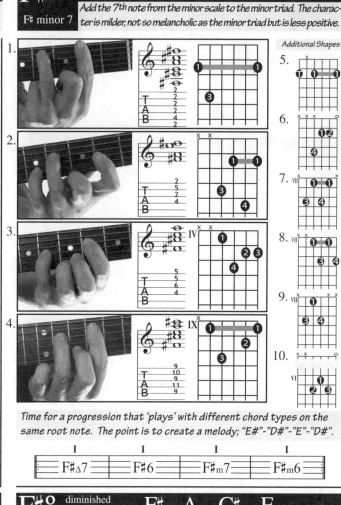

Additional Shapes

Time for a progression that 'plays' with different chord types on the same root note. The point is to create a melody; "E#"-"D#"-"E"-"D#".

I	I	I	I
F#∆7	F#6	F#m7	F#m6

F#m9 — F# - A - C# - (E) - C#

F#m9 and F#m add9 — The shapes of 'm9' and 'm add 9' are similar but the sound of the 'm add9' chord is more 'mystic' than 'm9', as it omits the 7th.

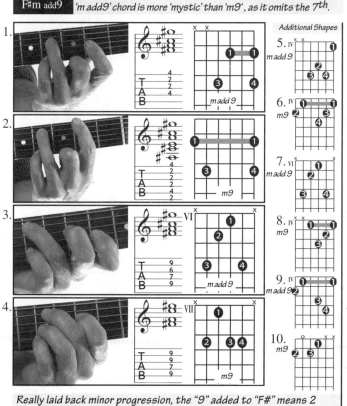

Additional Shapes

Really laid back minor progression, the "9" added to "F#" means 2 notes fall in parallel "G#" to "F#" and "C#" to "B", interesting.

I	IV	VII	V
F#m9	B	F°7	C#7

F#° — diminished group — F# - A - C# - E

F#°, F#°7 & F#m7b5 — Diminished chords have similar fingerings and uses, the m7b5 adds a minor 7th and for °7 flatten the minor 7th another fret.

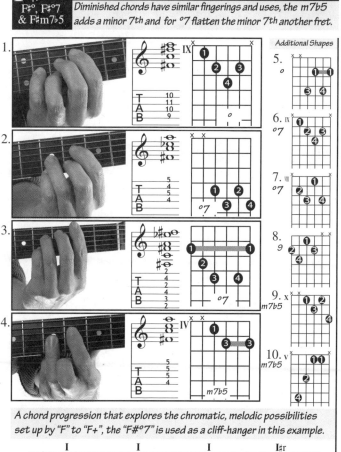

Additional Shapes

A chord progression that explores the chromatic, melodic possibilities set up by "F" to "F+", the "F#°7" is used as a cliff-hanger in this example.

I	I	I	I#r
F	F+	F6	F#°7

43

F♯6 — F♯ - A♯ - C♯ - D♯
F♯ Six

Add the sixth note of the major scale to the major triad. An instantly uplifting chord, some shapes sound like "m7", keep 6th high up in chord.

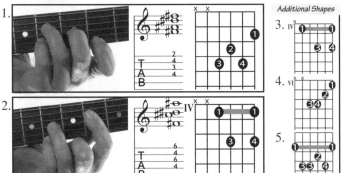

Additional Shapes
3. IV
4. VI
5.

Chord progression given the 'lighten it up with an added 6" treatment. Does give an immediate new angle to these well worn chords.

I	VI	II	V
F♯6	D♯m7	G♯m7	C♯7

F♯6/9 — F♯ - A♯ - C♯ - D♯ - G♯
F♯ six nine

Add the 6th and 9th notes from major scale to major triad. Strange exotic blend of sounds can link unlikely chords together.

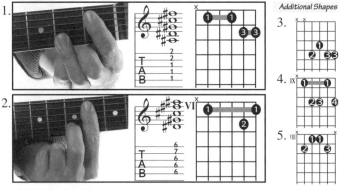

Additional Shapes
3.
4. IX
5. VIII

An example of how you can slickly manage key changes by using chord extensions to smooth and disguise i.e. "F♯6/9 to "AΔ7".

I	III	IV	V7
F♯6/9	AΔ7	Bm9	C♯7

F♯sus4 — F♯ - B - C♯
F♯ suspended 4th

A major triad that has the 4th note of scale 'suspended' over the 3rd. A tense sound that is resolved by releasing 4th and hearing the 3rd.

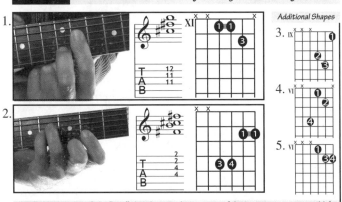

Additional Shapes
3. IX
4. VI
5. VI

Really classy use of the "sus" chord, notice how you can (playing as open as possible) keep 2 notes from "DΔ7" for "F♯sus", then keep 2 from this for the "Bm7" - nice.

IV	VI	II	V
DΔ7	F♯sus	Bm7	E7

F♯5 — F♯ - C♯ - (F♯)
F5 (no 3rd) 'Power chord'

Take the 3rd out of any major/minor triad and you have a "5" chord. Most effective with loud electric playing, saves worrying about keys.

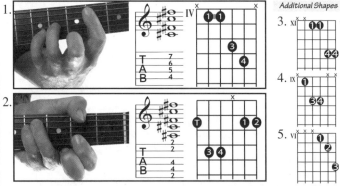

Additional Shapes
3. XI
4. IX
5. VI

This shows how well power chords can mix in with fuller sounding chords. The "B add9" brings "D♯" and "F♯" to the party - anticipating chords yet to come.

I	IV	III	V
F♯5	Badd9	A5	C♯5

F♯13 — F♯ - A♯ - C♯ - E - G♯ - (B) - D♯
F♯ 13

13 chord 'should' contain all the above notes, in practice the 7th and 13th (=6th) are essential, the 9th richer, 11th unused. An exotic.

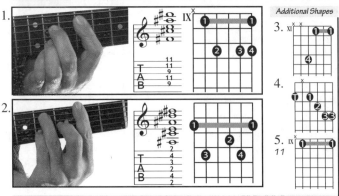

Additional Shapes
3. XI
4.
5. IX
11

Bored by the most obvious variant of the 3 chord trick; "I"-"IV"-"V", try this one, notice how you only have to move one finger to change from "F♯13" to "BbΔ7".

I	I	IV	V
F♯13	F♯13	BΔ7	C♯7

F♯+ — F♯ - A♯ - C## (=D)
F♯ Augmented

Take a major triad and sharpen the 5th by 1 fret. Often used after the major, the sharp 5th progressing 1 fret at a time to next chord.

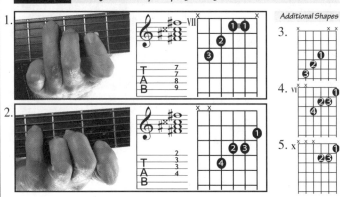

Additional Shapes
3.
4. VI
5. X

This is a neat way of sprucing up two mainstay chords. Notice that all you do to change from "F♯+" to "BmΔ7" is add the "B" root.

I	I	IV	IV
F♯	F♯+	BmΔ7	BΔ7

F#m6   F# - A - C# - D#
F# minor six   Add the 6th from the major scale to a minor triad. The 6th is commonly added to the triad to give a 2nd note in common with next chord.

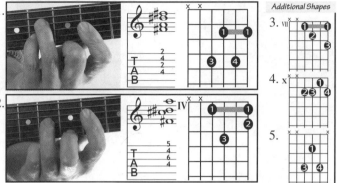

Nice angle on some fairly well worn chords. The extensions on each chord intentionally added to give an additional common note with the following chord.

II	I	V	III7
F#m6	E∆7	Badd9	G#7sus

F#m ∆7   F# - A - C# - E# (=F)
F# minor major 7   Add the 7th from the major scale to a minor triad. Rarely used on its own. Usually follows either "m7", "m" or "m6". Similar to augmented.

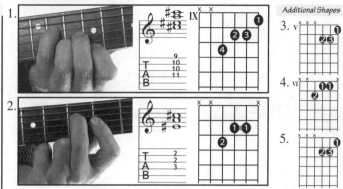

A progression that shows the attractive melody created by "m" to "m∆7" to "m7". There are a number of options for last chord, here the "IV 9".

I	I	I	IV
F#m	F#m∆7	F#m7	B9

F#7sus4   F# - B - C# - E
F# seven suspended 4th   With a flat (minor) 7th AND a suspended 4th this chord is over-loaded with tension. Sometimes used in place of the "11" chord.

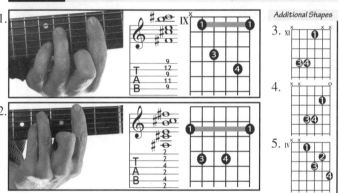

Typical strong minor progresion where the main surprise is that the "F#7sus" doesn't resolve to plain "F#7". The effect is that B is less convincing as the "I".

I	VI	IV	V
Bm	A	E7	F#7sus

F#7#9   F# - A# - C# - E - G## (=A)
F# seven sharp nine   Wickedly tense, a regular 7 chord with a sharp 9th (equal to sticking a minor 3rd on top). Usually on either 5th or 1st notes of the scale.

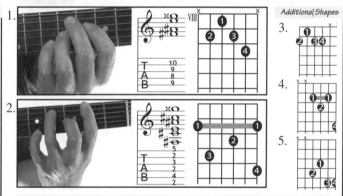

A progression that sees the "7#9" chord in the "I" position. A great tension device broken up here by good use of power chords on "IV" & "V".

V	IV	I	V	IV	I
C#5	B5	F#7#9	C#5	B5	F#7#9

F#m13   F# - A - C# - E - G# - (B) - D#
F# minor 13   "m13" 'should' contain all above notes but often omits 9th and 11th. The "m11" is also quite common and has 11th but no 13th.

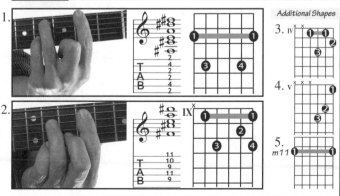

A progression that could be in either E major or the relative minor C#. The 13 is added to "F#" to link more smoothly to B7 however, its character takes over.

VI	I	II	V
C#m	E	F#m13	B7

F#-5   F# - A# - C
F# Flat 5   Another tension chord that has a powerful need to resolve to the major chord.

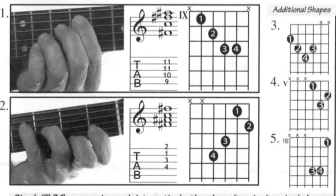

Simple "I"-"V" progression made interesting by the release/tension/tension/release idea. "F#-5" leads to "C#" with a similar effect to a "sus" chord.

I	I	V	V
F#	F#-5	C#sus	C#

45

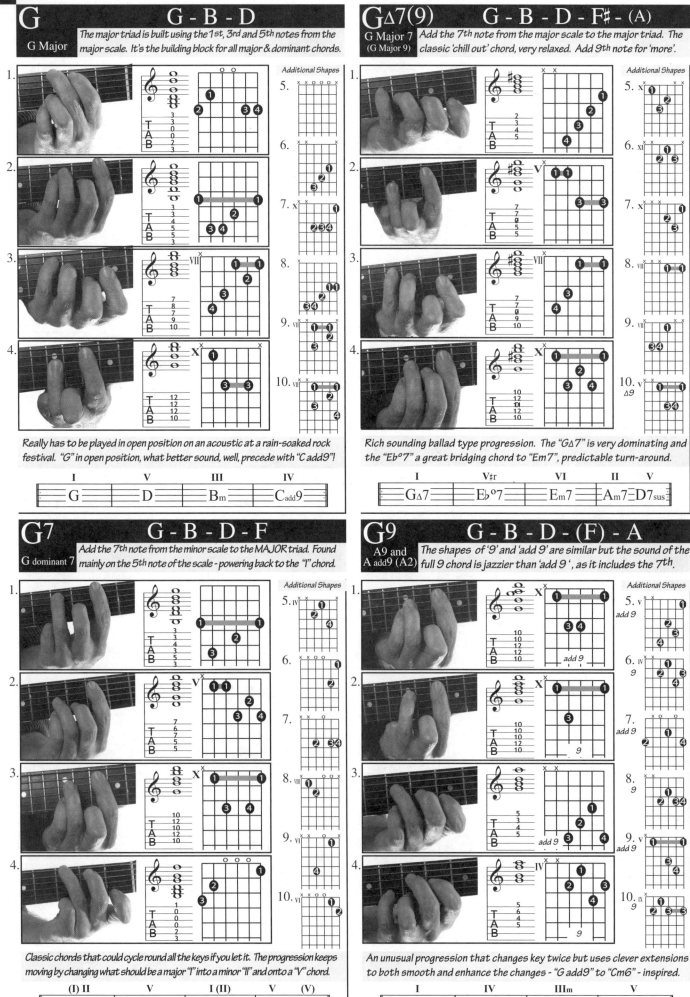

G

G — G-B-D

G Major

The major triad is built using the 1st, 3rd and 5th notes from the major scale. It's the building block for all major & dominant chords.

Additional Shapes

Really has to be played in open position on an acoustic at a rain-soaked rock festival. "G" in open position, what better sound, well, precede with "Cadd9"!

I	V	III	IV
G	D	Bm	Cadd9

G△7(9) — G-B-D-F♯-(A)

G Major 7
(G Major 9)

Add the 7th note from the major scale to the major triad. The classic 'chill out' chord, very relaxed. Add 9th note for 'more'.

Additional Shapes

Rich sounding ballad type progression. The "G△7" is very dominating and the "Eb°7" a great bridging chord to "Em7", predictable turn-around.

I	V#r	VI	II	V
G△7	Eb°7	Em7	Am7	D7sus

G7 — G-B-D-F

G dominant 7

Add the 7th note from the minor scale to the MAJOR triad. Found mainly on the 5th note of the scale - powering back to the "I" chord.

Additional Shapes

Classic chords that could cycle round all the keys if you let it. The progression keeps moving by changing what should be a major "I" into a minor "II" and onto a "V" chord.

(I) II	V	I (II)	V	(V)
Dm7	G7	Cm7	F7	A7

G9 — G-B-D-(F)-A

A9 and
A add9 (A2)

The shapes of '9' and 'add 9' are similar but the sound of the full 9 chord is jazzier than 'add 9', as it includes the 7th.

Additional Shapes

An unusual progression that changes key twice but uses clever extensions to both smooth and enhance the changes - "Gadd9" to "Cm6" - inspired.

I	IV	IIIm	V
Gadd9	Cm6	Bbm13	D7

46

Gm — G - B♭ - D

G Minor

The minor triad is built using the 1st, 3rd and 5th notes from the minor scale. It's the building block for all minor chords.

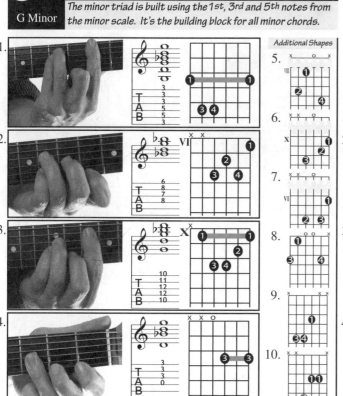

Great and different minor progression. Gm is always strong in this position the "9" on the "IV" (C) chord is a great idea, leading to "D sus".

I	III	IV9	V	V
Gm	B♭	C9	Dsus	D

Gm7 — G - B♭ - D - F

G Minor 7

Add the 7th note from the minor scale to the minor triad. The character is milder, not so melancholic as the minor triad but is less positive.

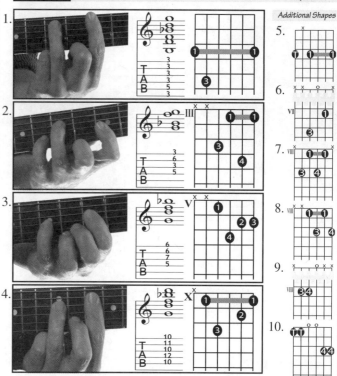

Quite unusual to progress in the minor mode; "I"-"II"-"V". The "II" chord does modulate slightly but the two "m7" chords together form a good bond.

I	II	V	V
Gm7	Am7	D	D9

Gm9 — G - B♭ - D - (F) - A

Gm9 and Gm add9

The shapes of 'm9' and 'm add 9' are similar but the sound of the 'm add9' chord is more 'mystic' than 'm9', as it omits the 7th.

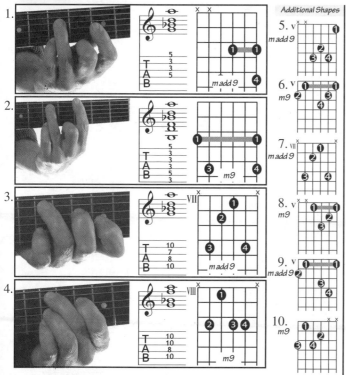

You'll be rushing down to your nearest smokey jazz lounge bar after playing this one, Gm9 to E♭9 is amazing, very different sounding due to the key change taking place.

VI	IV	III	V
Gm9	E♭9	Dm9	F9

G° diminished group — G - B♭ - D♭ - (F(♭))

G°, G°7 & Gm7♭5

Diminished chords have similar fingerings and uses, the 'm7b5' adds a minor 7th and for °7 flatten the minor 7th another fret.

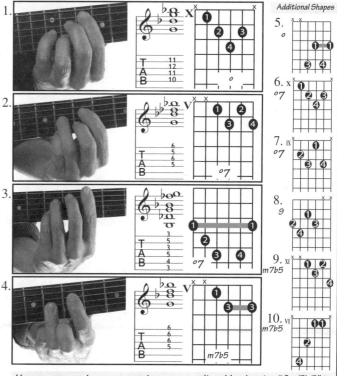

Very common minor progression, very predictable showing "Gm7b5" in its usual role on the "II" progressing to "V" in the minor mode.

I	IV	II	V
Fm7	B♭m7	Gm7♭5	C7

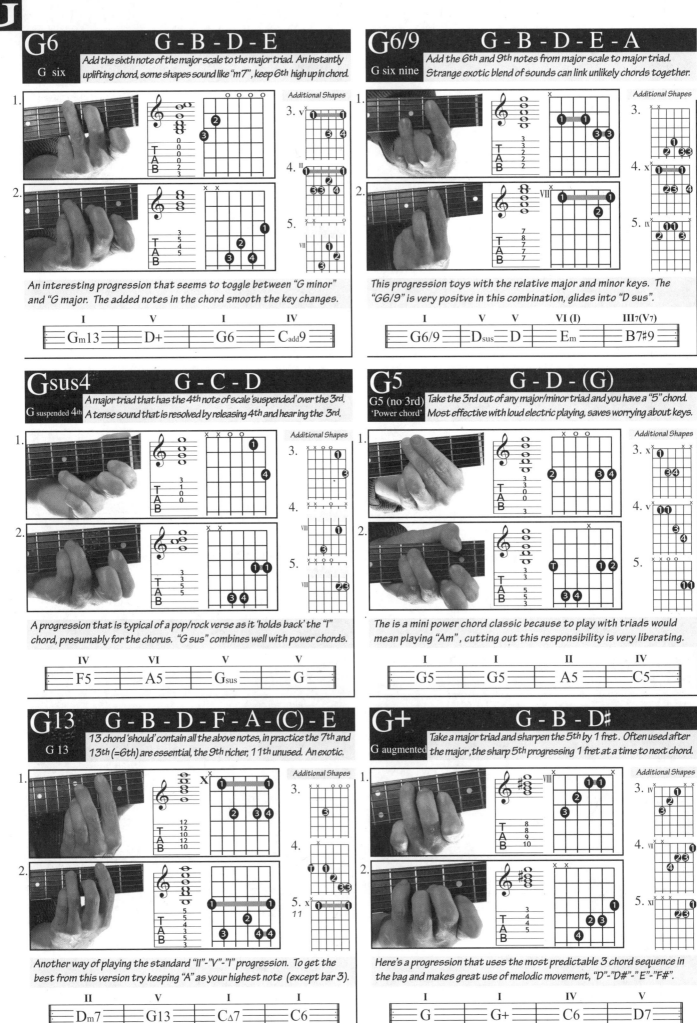

G6 — G - B - D - E

G six

Add the sixth note of the major scale to the major triad. An instantly uplifting chord, some shapes sound like "m7", keep 6th high up in chord.

Additional Shapes

An interesting progression that seems to toggle between "G minor" and "G major. The added notes in the chord smooth the key changes.

I	V	I	IV
Gm13	D+	G6	Cadd9

G6/9 — G - B - D - E - A

G six nine

Add the 6th and 9th notes from major scale to major triad. Strange exotic blend of sounds can link unlikely chords together.

Additional Shapes

This progression toys with the relative major and minor keys. The "G6/9" is very positve in this combination, glides into "D sus".

I	V	V	VI (I)	III7(V7)
G6/9	Dsus	D	Em	B7#9

Gsus4 — G - C - D

G suspended 4th

A major triad that has the 4th note of scale 'suspended' over the 3rd. A tense sound that is resolved by releasing 4th and hearing the 3rd.

Additional Shapes

A progression that is typical of a pop/rock verse as it 'holds back' the "I" chord, presumably for the chorus. "G sus" combines well with power chords.

IV	VI	V	V
F5	A5	Gsus	G

G5 — G - D - (G)

G5 (no 3rd)
'Power chord'

Take the 3rd out of any major/minor triad and you have a "5" chord. Most effective with loud electric playing, saves worrying about keys.

Additional Shapes

The is a mini power chord classic because to play with triads would mean playing "Am" , cutting out this responsibility is very liberating.

I	I	II	IV
G5	G5	A5	C5

G13 — G - B - D - F - A - (C) - E

G 13

13 chord 'should' contain all the above notes, in practice the 7th and 13th (=6th) are essential, the 9th richer, 11th unused. An exotic.

Additional Shapes

Another way of playing the standard "II"-"V"-"I" progression. To get the best from this version try keeping "A" as your highest note (except bar 3).

II	V	I	I
Dm7	G13	CΔ7	C6

G+ — G - B - D#

G augmented

Take a major triad and sharpen the 5th by 1 fret . Often used after the major , the sharp 5th progressing 1 fret at a time to next chord.

Additional Shapes

Here's a progression that uses the most predictable 3 chord sequence in the bag and makes great use of melodic movement, "D"-"D#"- "E"- "F#".

I	I	IV	V
G	G+	C6	D7

Gm6 — G - Bb - D - E
G minor 6
Add the 6th from the major scale to a minor triad. The 6th is commonly added to the triad to give a 2nd note in common with next chord.

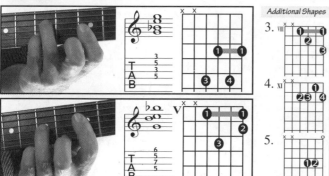

A great way to cut through a predictable minor chord progression and introduce natural melody; "G"(G)-"F#"-(GmΔ7)"F"(Gm7)-"E"(Gm6)-"Eb"(EbΔ7)-"D"(D).

I	I	I	I	VI	V
Gm	GmΔ7	Gm7	Gm6	EbΔ7	D7

GmΔ7 — G - Bb - D - F#
G minor major 7
Add the 7th from the major scale to a minor triad. Rarely used on its own. Usually follows either "m7", "m" or "m6". Similar to augmented.

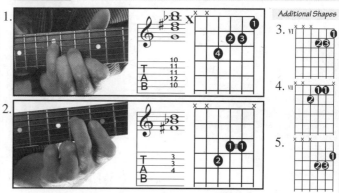

A very unusual sequence that shows "mΔ7" in its suspense role, like an augmented chord in suspense; tension, release, tension, release - to put it mildly.

III+/VII	VI	III+/VII	II
GmΔ7	Fm7	GmΔ7	Bbm7

G7sus4 — G - C - D - F
G seven suspended 4th
With a flat (minor) 7th AND a suspended 4th this chord is overloaded with tension. Sometimes used in place of the "11" chord.

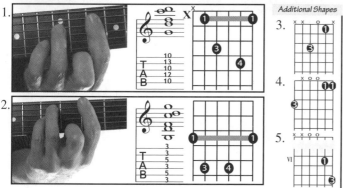

Classic chord sequence in a massive disguise. Lots of cheery extensions give this progression a sort of Brazilian carnival flavour.

I	VI	II	V
C6	Am9	Dm13	G7sus

G7#9 — G - B - D - F - A#
G7 sharp 9
Wickedly tense, a regular 7 chord with a sharp 9th (equal to sticking a minor 3rd on top). Usually on either 5th or 1st notes of the scale.

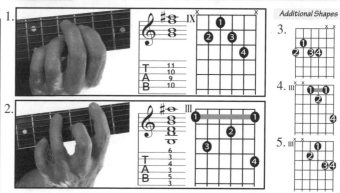

"7#9" is an absolutely awesome sound when played in the "V" position. When it's the minor "V" as here, seems to be even better.

I	IV	I	V
Cm	Fm	Cm	G7#9

Gm13 — G - Bb - D - F - A - (C) - E
G minor 13
"m13" 'should' contain all above notes but often omits 9th and 11th. The "m11" is also quite common and has 11th but no 13th.

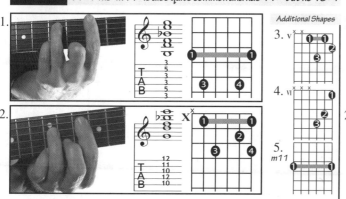

A classic "II"-"V"-"I" progression with a twist. Rich extensions give this version a lively fresh appeal and the "D7" acts as a 'V' giving the "Gm13" greater importance.

II (I)	V	I	VI7 (V)
Gm13	C7	F6	D7

G-5 — G - B - Db
G flat 5
Another tension chord that has a powerful need to resolve to the major chord.

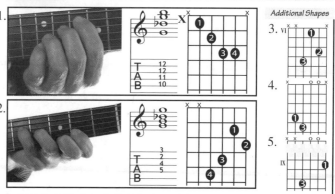

Simple chords that play with the possibilities of adding different tension devices to a "G" root. First, "flat 5", second "sus" - similar role.

I	I	I	V
G	G-5	Gsus	D7

Ab
Ab Major

Ab – C – Eb

The major triad is built using the 1st, 3rd and 5th notes from the major scale. It's the building block for all major & dominant chords.

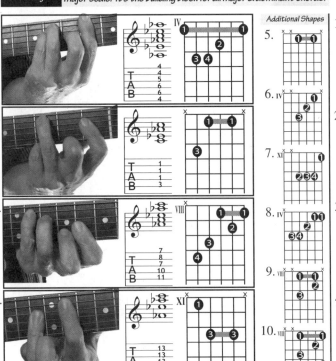

Additional Shapes

Common in rock music this progression sees "Ab" in seemingly the wrong place for a major chord on "III". Very powerful but mainly rock.

II△	V	IV	II△	V	IV
F	Bb	Ab	F	Bb	Ab

Ab△7(9)
Ab Major 7
Ab Major 9

Ab – C – Eb – G (Bb)

Add the 7th note from the major scale to the major triad. The classic 'chill out' chord, very relaxed. Add 9th note for 'more'.

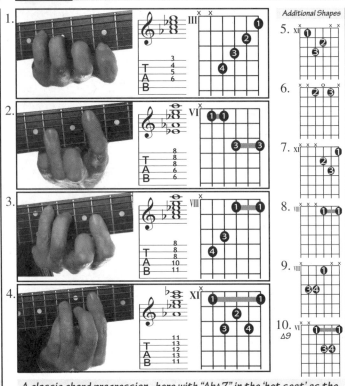

Additional Shapes

A classic chord progression, here with "Ab△7" in the 'hot seat' as the "i" chord. It's always a great sound "7" on the "III" could go to "Fm".

I	II	V	III7
Ab△7	Bbm7	Eb	C7

Ab7
Ab dominant 7

Ab – C – Eb – Gb

Add the 7th note from the minor scale to the MAJOR triad. Found mainly on the 5th note of the scale - powering back to the "I" chord.

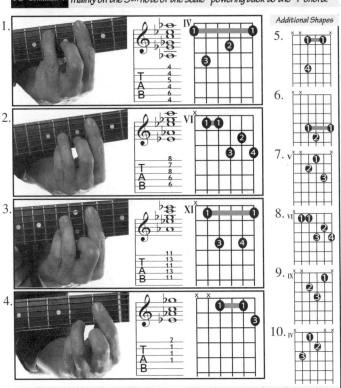

Additional Shapes

Great combination of "7" chords, the key changes with each chord yet the progression ensures "Ab7" will eventually rule strength wise.

I	VII (I)	IV	VI (V)
Ab7	G7	C7	Eb7

Ab9
Ab 9 and
Ab add9 (Ab2)

Ab – C – Eb – (Gb) – Bb

The shapes of '9' and 'add 9' are similar but the sound of the full 9 chord is jazzier than 'add 9', as it includes the 7th.

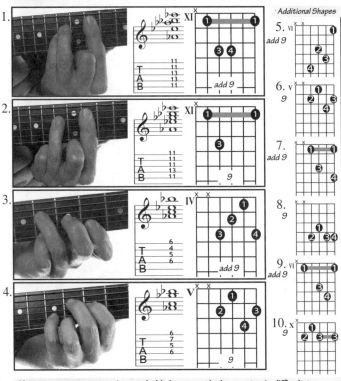

Additional Shapes

Not a common progression, probably because the key centre is difficult to determine and therefore doesn't resolve. "Ab9" sounds different in this role.

II	I	IVm	V
Bbm7	Ab9	Dbm6	Eb7

Abm — Ab - Cb - Eb
Ab Minor — The minor triad is built using the 1st, 3rd and 5th notes from the minor scale. It's the building block for all minor chords.

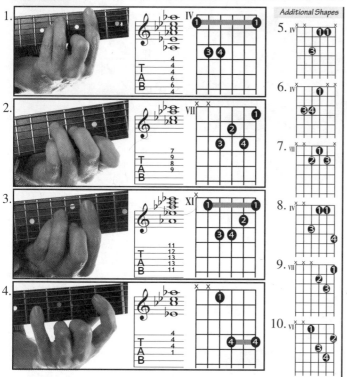

Great progression, starts in E major goes to the "III" minor chord which changes to "7" so changing the key to C# minor, then "B7" changes it back to E major again.

I	III	III#3 (V)	(I) VI	V
E	G#m	G#7	C#m	B7

Abm7 — Ab - Cb - Eb - Gb
Ab minor 7 — Add the 7th note from the minor scale to the minor triad. The character is milder, not so melancholic as the minor triad but is less positive.

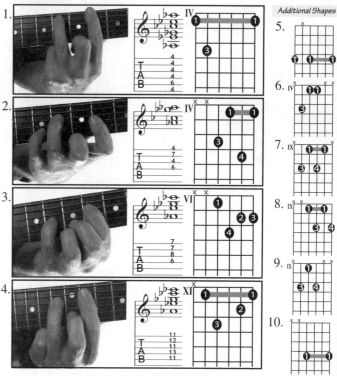

Typical minor progression, use of "m7" chords, even on the "V" which can be "7", keeps the progression gentle, but leaves it drifting - pretty.

I	VI	V	IV
G#m7	EΔ7	D#m7	C#m7

Abm9 — Ab - Cb - Eb - (Gb) - Bb
Abm9 and Abm add9 — The shapes of 'm9' and 'm add 9' are similar but the sound of the 'm add9' chord is more 'mystic' than 'm9', as it omits the 7th.

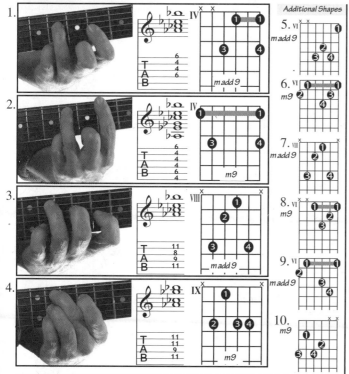

A pretty weird progression that changes key when it feels like it and doesn't use a pivotal chord to focus on the key centre - interesting.

VIIm	bIIm	III	V7
Abm9	Bm7	Db9	F7

Ab° diminished group — Ab - C - Eb - (Gb(b))
Ab°, Ab°7 & Abm7b5 — Diminished chords have similar fingerings and uses, the 'm7b5' adds a minor 7th and for °7 flatten the minor 7th another fret.

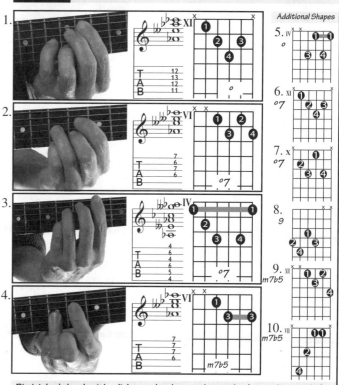

Diminished chords either link two chords together or they're used instead of the "V7" as here. As both are played in the progression you'll hear the contrast.

I	#VII	I	V
Am	G#°7	Am	E7

51

A♭6   A♭ - C - E♭ - F

A♭ Six

Add the sixth note of the major scale to the major triad. An instantly uplifting chord, some shapes sound like "m7", keep 6th high up in chord.

Additional Shapes

A really nice minor progression, the "6" is obviously added to the "Ab" to keep continuity with the previous "F" chord and the following "Bb" chord.

I	III	IV	V
Fm	A♭6	B♭m7	C7

A♭6/9   A♭ - C - E♭ - F - B♭

A♭ six nine

Add the 6th and 9th notes from major scale to major triad. Strange exotic blend of sounds can link unlikely chords together.

Additional Shapes

Unusual progression that's in E major but starts out of key. This actually shows off what an amazing sounding chord the 6/9 is; to "E6" great change.

III	I	II	V
G♯6/9	E6	F♯m7	B2

A♭sus4   A♭ - D♭ - E♭

A♭ suspended 4th

A major triad that has the 4th note of scale 'suspended' over the 3rd. A tense sound that is resolved by releasing 4th and hearing the 3rd.

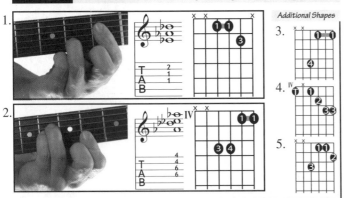

Additional Shapes

If you've got a simple progression and you want to keep it simple, "sus" chord to the rescue it realy makes this progression come alive.

I	IV	I	I
A♭	D♭	A♭	A♭sus

A♭5   A♭ - E♭ - (A♭)

A♭5 (no 3rd) 'Power chord'

Take the 3rd out of any major/minor triad and you have a "5" chord. Most effective with loud electric playing, saves worrying about keys.

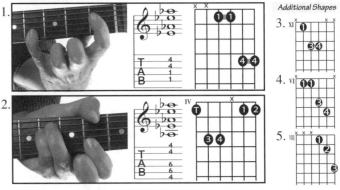

Additional Shapes

You won't hear this little gem very often but any chord that is fascinating on it's own, tends to combine well with power chords - as here.

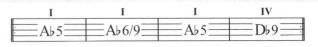

I	I	I	IV
A♭5	A♭6/9	A♭5	D♭9

A♭13   A♭ - C - E♭ - G♭ - B♭ - (D♭) - F

A♭ 13

13 chord 'should' contain all the above notes, in practice the 7th and 13th (=6th) are essential, the 9th richer, 11th unused. An exotic.

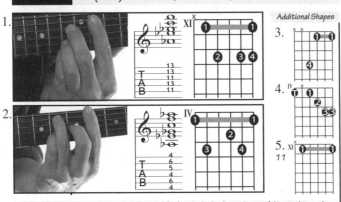

Additional Shapes

This classic progression is given a lift (and slight key change) by making the "I" chord "13". The upside is that the progression is immediately vibrant.

I	VI	II	V
A♭13	Fm	B♭m	E♭7

A♭+   A♭ - C - E

A♭ Augmented

Take a major triad and sharpen the 5th by 1 fret. Often used after the major, the sharp 5th progressing 1 fret at a time to next chord.

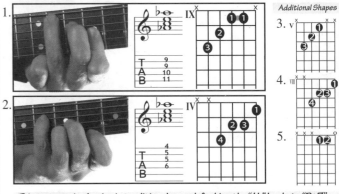

Additional Shapes

This progression begins in traditional enough fashion the "Ab" leads to "DΔ7" courtesy of "Ab+" and instead of peaking on Eb goes to "Bb7" - a bit different.

I	I	IV	II7
A♭	A♭+	D♭Δ7	B♭7

Abm6   Ab - Cb - Eb - F

Ab Minor six — Add the 6th from the major scale to a minor triad. The 6th is commonly added to the triad to give a 2nd note in common with next chord.

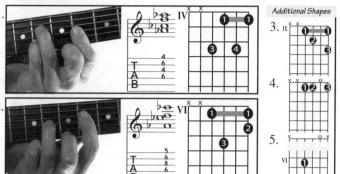

Really interesting progression with some wicked changes; "Bb7sus" to "Abm6" - wow, as is "E7" to "Bb7sus" on the repeat.

II	I	IV	VI7
Bb7sus	Abm6	Dbm	E7

Abm△7   Ab - Cb - Eb - G

Ab minor major seven — Add the 7th from the major scale to a minor triad. Rarely used on its own. Usually follows either "m7", "m" or "m6". Similar to augmented.

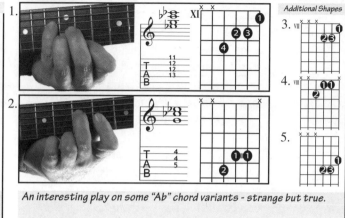

An interesting play on some "Ab" chord variants - strange but true.

I	I	I	I#r
Abm△7	Ab△7	Abm△7	Am7b5

Ab7sus4   Ab - Db - Eb - Gb

Ab seven suspended 4th — With a flat (minor) 7th AND a suspended 4th this chord is over-loaded with tension. Sometimes used in place of the "11" chord.

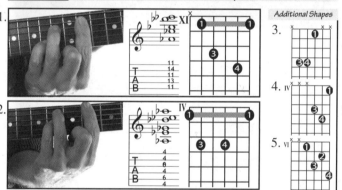

A very popular progression, quite easy to play. Notice how by not resolving the "sus7" to "7" a degree of tension or uncertainty hangs over the "i" chord.

I	III	IV	V
Db	Fm	Gb	Ab7sus

Ab7#9   Ab - C - Eb - Gb - B

Ab seven sharp nine — Wickedly tense, a regular 7 chord with a sharp 9th (equal to sticking a minor 3rd on top). Usually on either 5th or 1st notes of the scale.

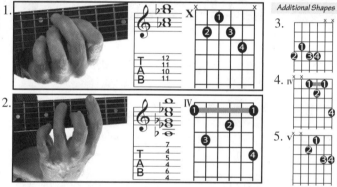

The key changes somewhat unpredictably at first, but the final tension vamp on the "V" chord, comparing "7b5" with "7#9" is amazing.

VII	VI	V	V
Bm	A13	Abm7b5	Ab7#9

Abm13   Ab - Cb - Eb - Gb - Bb - (Db) - F

Ab minor 13 — "m13" 'should' contain all above notes but often omits 9th and 11th. The "m11" is also quite common and has 11th but no 13th.

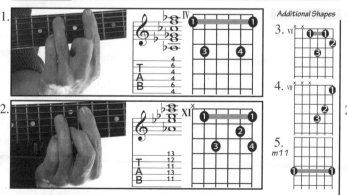

A pretty strange progression but as with many progressions with unpredictable key changes there's never a dull moment - spend some time finding the right shapes.

I	VI	II	bII7
Abm13	E	Bbsus	A7

Ab-5   Ab - C - Ebb (=D)

Ab flat 5 — Another tension chord that has a powerful need to resolve to the major chord.

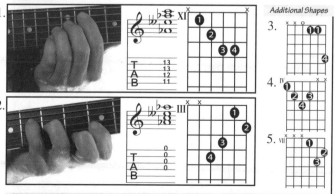

Always good for a long verse, alternating between the major "I" chord and the minor "VI" chord. The "flat 5" is there like a "sus" chord to create some danger or tension.

I	VI	I	I
Ab	Fm	Ab	Ab-5

GUITAR CHORD HEAVEN - UNDERSTANDING THE CD

To get the full benefit of the accompanying CD please take a few moments to read the notes for any track you're going to listen to , or play along to. There are no count-ins as such, simply use the first sequence as your count-in. Each track will repeat the sequence many times so there is plenty of time. During the course of all tracks on the CD you should hear all chord types described in the book in a number of different roles. Each track is intended to specifically demonstrate a 'featured' chord.

Start by listening to each track and identifying which chord is which by counting along and looking at the progression as detailed below. As the tracks are produced to be fun to play along to, beginners may find it hard to identify each chord at first. If you are new to playing music you must start by counting along to the track until you are completely sure which chord is which and are confident that you can hear where each chord changes. Generally, chord changes are made each bar, which should make this process quite easy. The main

rhythm guitar track is produced fairly loud, slightly to one side of the stereo image which should enable you to listen precisely to the chord shapes outlined in the track details below. Once you're confident you can identify each chord and where the chords change you can begin to play along.

Begin by practising each chord shape used. If you are a beginner this may take some time - don't give up - keep practising and you'll soon get it. Practise each change slowly so that you can see and understand what the hand has to do to change chord. When you can play each shape - in time - slowly , begin to speed up - little by little. Soon you'll be able to join in with the track.

Soloing to each track is great fun. The lead solo is slightly to one side of the stereo image and so although you can't lose it completely you can turn it down a bit, so that you can solo over the top yourself. If you need more help learning guitar see the back page for details of our excellent tutor books and videos.

CD tracks 1-20 - chord types. CD tracks 21-41 - play-alongs

The following tracks demonstrate every photographed chord beginning on E. So you'll need pages 34-37 ready.

Track 1 - MAJOR △
E Major triad - 4 shapes

Track 6 - m7
E Minor seven - 4 shapes

Track 11 - sus4 (sus)
E suspended 4 - 2 shapes

Track 16 - m△7
E Minor major 7 - 2 shapes

Track 2 - MAJOR 7
E Major seven - 4 shapes

Track 7 - m9 & m add9
Em add9 (1 and 3) Em9 (2 and 4)

Track 12 - 5
E five - 'power chord' - 2 shapes

Track 17 - 7sus4
E seven suspended 4 - x2

Track 3 - 7
E dominant seven - 4 shapes

Track 8 - °, °7 & m7♭5
E diminished, diminished 7 (2 & 3), minor 7♭5

Track 13 - 13
E thirteen - 2 shapes

Track 18 - 7#9
E seven sharp nine - 2 shapes

Track 4 - 9 and add9
E add 9 (1 and 3) E9 (2 and 4)

Track 9 - 6
E Six - 2 shapes

Track 14 - +, +5 AUG.
E Augmented (sharp 5 or plus 5)

Track 19 - m13
E Minor thirteen - 2 shapes

Track 5 - MINOR m
E Minor triad - 4 shapes

Track 10 - 6/9
E6/9 - 2 shapes

Track 15 - m6
E Minor six - 2 shapes

Track 20 - -5 (♭5)
E flat 5 - 2 shapes

Track 21 - FEATURED CHORD = MAJOR
All chords are major - classic 3 chord trick stuff ; I - IV - I - V .
This track sounds easy but - because we thought you'd enjoy play-

ing ALL the major chords the music is in four different keys - make sure you know ALL the chords before you begin! Also beware if you want to solo as the key changes will give you plenty to think about.

F   B♭   C   A♭   D♭   E♭   B   E   F#   D   G   A

The above chords show all shapes used. The progression for each key is as follows: 1 bar on each F - B♭ - F - B♭ - F - B♭ - C - C. Move up 3 frets and repeat.

Track 22 - FEATURED CHORD = MAJOR SEVEN △7
A: Major 7 chord is in 'passing' on bar 2. B: Major 7 on both bars IV -I.
Section A: 4 beats on each chord. D - D△7 - D7 , then 2 beats on G and A. x2

D | D△7 | D7 | G | A || G△7 | D△7 |
Section B: 4 beats on each chord: G△7 - D△7, repeat 3 times then G△7 - A. Back to A.

Track 24 - FEATURED CHORD = Add 9
Classic I - VI - IV - V progression given both 'indie' and classic treatment.
Section A & C: 2 styles - same chords; 4 beats per chord C5-A5-F5-G5.

C5   A5   F5   G5   Cadd9   Dadd9   G5
Section B: demonstrates the 'hollow' sound of 'add9' chords; Cadd9, Dadd9 & G5.

Track 23 - FEATURED CHORD = Dominant 7 "7"
One section 12 bar blues which is a classic three chord trick (I - IV - V)
The standard 12 bar (4 beats on each chord) I-I-I-I-IV-IV-I-I-V-IV-I-V.

G7v1   G7v2   G7v3 | C7v1   C7v2   C7v3 | D7v1   D7v2   D7v3
In key of G: G-G-G-G-C-C-G-G-D-C-G-D, repeat. 3 versions per chord. V1, V2 x2 - V3 .

Track 25 - FEATURED CHORD = Dominant 9 "9"
Mostly a D9 / C#9 vamp, these "9" chords are just instantly funky!
Section A: Chop chords short with D9 interrupted by C#9 on beat 2+.

D9   C#9   D9   Gm7   D   A
Section B: Shows D9 setting up a sweet progression: D9-Gm7-D-A; 4 beats each.

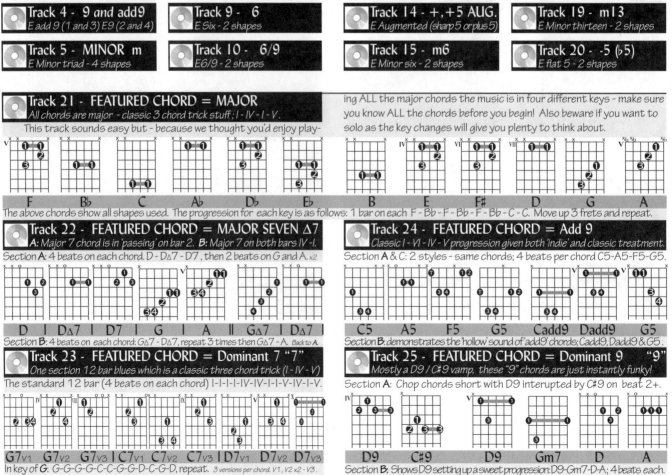

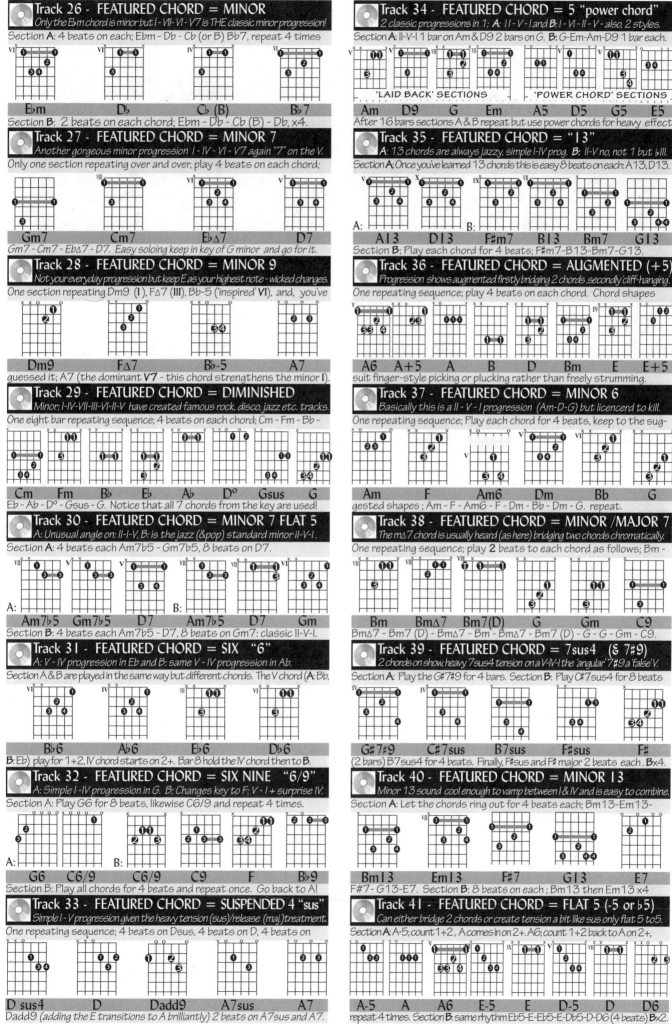

Track 26 - FEATURED CHORD = MINOR
Only the Ebm chord is minor but I - VII- VI- V7 is THE classic minor progression!
Section A: 4 beats on each; Ebm - Db - Cb (or B) Bb7, repeat 4 times

| Ebm | Db | Cb (B) | Bb7 |

Section B: 2 beats on each chord; Ebm - Db - Cb (B) - Db, x4.

Track 27 - FEATURED CHORD = MINOR 7
Another gorgeous minor progression I - IV - VI - V7 again "7" on the V.
Only one section repeating over and over, play 4 beats on each chord;

| Gm7 | Cm7 | Eb△7 | D7 |

Gm7 - Cm7 - Eb△7 - D7. Easy soloing keep in key of G minor and go for it.

Track 28 - FEATURED CHORD = MINOR 9
Not your everyday progression but keep E as your highest note - wicked changes.
One section repeating Dm9 (I), F△7 (III), Bb-5 ('inspired' VI), and, you've

| Dm9 | F△7 | Bb-5 | A7 |

guessed it; A7 (the dominant V7 - this chord strengthens the minor I).

Track 29 - FEATURED CHORD = DIMINISHED
Minor; I-IV-VII-III-VI-II-V have created famous rock, disco, jazz etc. tracks.
One eight bar repeating sequence; 4 beats on each chord; Cm - Fm - Bb -

| Cm | Fm | Bb | Eb | Ab | Do | Gsus | G |

Eb - Ab - Do - Gsus - G. Notice that all 7 chords from the key are used!

Track 30 - FEATURED CHORD = MINOR 7 FLAT 5
A: Unusual angle on: II-I-V, B: is the jazz (&pop) standard minor ii-V-I.
Section A: 4 beats each Am7b5 - Gm7b5, 8 beats on D7.

A: | Am7b5 | Gm7b5 | D7 | B: | Am7b5 | D7 | Gm |

Section B: 4 beats each Am7b5 - D7, 8 beats on Gm7: classic II-V-I.

Track 31 - FEATURED CHORD = SIX "6"
A: V - IV progression in Eb and B: same V - IV progression in Ab.
Section A & B are played in the same way but different chords. The V chord (A: Bb,

| Bb6 | Ab6 | Eb6 | Db6 |

B: Eb) play for 1+2, IV chord starts on 2+. Bar 8 hold the IV chord then to B.

Track 32 - FEATURED CHORD = SIX NINE "6/9"
A: Simple I -IV progression in G. B: Changes key to F; V - I + surprise IV.
Section A: Play G6 for 8 beats, likewise C6/9 and repeat 4 times.

A: | G6 | C6/9 | C6/9 | C9 | B: | F | Bb9 |

Section B: Play all chords for 4 beats and repeat once. Go back to A!

Track 33 - FEATURED CHORD = SUSPENDED 4 "sus"
Simple I - V progression given the heavy tension (sus)/release (maj.) treatment.
One repeating sequence; 4 beats on Dsus, 4 beats on D, 4 beats on

| D sus4 | D | Dadd9 | A7sus | A7 |

Dadd9 (adding the E transitions to A brilliantly) 2 beats on A7sus and A7.

Track 34 - FEATURED CHORD = 5 "power chord"
2 classic progressions in 1; A: II - V - I and B: I - Vi - II - V - also, 2 styles.
Section A: II-V-I 1 bar on Am & D9 2 bars on G. B: G-Em-Am-D9 1 bar each.

'LAID BACK' SECTIONS | 'POWER CHORD' SECTIONS

| Am | D9 | G | Em | A5 | D5 | G5 | E5 |

After 16 bars sections A & B repeat but use power chords for heavy effect.

Track 35 - FEATURED CHORD = "13"
A: 13 chords are always jazzy, simple I-IV prog. B: II-V no, not I but bIII.
Section A: Once you've learned 13 chords this is easy 8 beats on each: A13, D13.

A: | A13 | D13 | F#m7 | B13 | B: | Bm7 | G13 |

Section B; Play each chord for 4 beats; F#m7-B13-Bm7-G13.

Track 36 - FEATURED CHORD = AUGMENTED (+5)
Progression shows augmented firstly bridging 2 chords, secondly cliff-hanging.
One repeating sequence; play 4 beats on each chord. Chord shapes

| A6 | A+5 | A | B | D | Bm | E | E+5 |

suit finger-style picking or plucking rather than freely strumming.

Track 37 - FEATURED CHORD = MINOR 6
Basically this is a II - V - I progression (Am-D-G) but licencerd to kill.
One repeating sequence; Play each chord for 4 beats, keep to the sug-

| Am | F | Am6 | Dm | Bb | G |

gested shapes ; Am - F - Am6 - F - Dm - Bb - Dm - G. repeat.

Track 38 - FEATURED CHORD = MINOR /MAJOR 7
The m△7 chord is usually heard (as here) bridging two chords chromatically.
One repeating sequence; play 2 beats to each chord as follows; Bm -

| Bm | Bm△7 | Bm7(D) | G | Gm | C9 |

Bm△7 - Bm7 (D) - Bm△7 - Bm - Bm△7 - Bm7 (D) - G - G - Gm - C9.

Track 39 - FEATURED CHORD = 7sus4 (& 7#9)
2 chords on show, heavy 7sus4 tension on a V-IV-I the 'angular' 7#9 a false' V.
Section A: Play the G#7#9 for 4 bars. Section B: Play C#7sus4 for 8 beats

| G#7#9 | C#7sus | B7sus | F#sus | F# |

(2 bars) B7sus4 for 4 beats. Finally, F#sus and F# major 2 beats each . Bx4.

Track 40 - FEATURED CHORD = MINOR 13
Minor 13 sound cool enough to vamp between I & IV and is easy to combine.
Section A: Let the chords ring out for 4 beats each; Bm13-Em13-

| Bm13 | Em13 | F#7 | G13 | E7 |

F#7 - G13-E7. Section B: 8 beats on each ; Bm13 then Em13 x4

Track 41 - FEATURED CHORD = FLAT 5 (-5 or b5)
Can either bridge 2 chords or create tension a bit like sus only flat 5 to5.
Section A: A-5; count 1+2, A comes in on 2+. A6; count 1+2 back to A on 2+,

| A-5 | A | A6 | E-5 | E | D-5 | D | D6 |

repeat 4 times. Section B: same rhythm Eb5-E-Eb5-E-Db5-D-D6 (4 beats) Bx2.

Also published by R & C Gregory Publishing Ltd

for *Guitar*

ISBN 1-901690-69-5

Guitar Chord Heaven is the ULTIMATE chord resource. 1680 chords with photos, diagrams, music and tab. PLUS over 270 chord progressions - spark off your creativity or understand more about chords and how they work. CD demonstrates important chord types, progressions and sounds.

ISBN 1-901690-15-6

"Learn Guitar From Beginner To Your 1st Band", by John A. MacLachlan. This book comes with a free CD produced to make you feel part of the band from day one. Technique, scales, chords, rhythm, reading music and realising your own creative potential are all made easy and fun. Also, things to watch out for when you join a band.

ISBN 1-901690-11-3

A Step By Step Guide To Everything You Need To Know About Being A Guitar Player, by John A. MacLachlan. This tutor book packs a punch of information to get you started in guitar playing. Loads of information and study tips for very little money.

for *Bass*

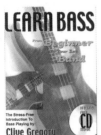

ISBN 1-901690-16-4

Learn Bass From Beginner To Your 1st Band, by Clive Gregory. This book comes with a free CD produced to make you feel part of the band from day one. 15 step tutor method with CD combines with all the information you need to learn bass.

ISBN 1-901690-09-1

A Great Way To Learn Bass, by Clive Gregory. Full of information covering; technique, scales, writing bass lines, groove and time-keeping, rhythm and things to watch out for when you join a band.

ISBN 1-901690-20-2

Clive Gregory's Foundation Course For Bass Guitar. Probably the most thorough tutor book for beginners to intermediate students. Every topic from technique to improvisation, slap to composing bass lines is discussed at length.

for *Drums*

ISBN 1-901690-13-X

A Step By Step Guide To Everything You Need To Know About Being A Drummer, by Neil Martin. One of the best beginners' drum books on the planet - simple, fun and very informative.

for *Keyboards*

ISBN 1-901690-12-1

A Step By Step Guide To Everything You Need To Know About Being A Keyboard Player, by Geoff Ellwood. Learn about scales, chords, keys, technique and how to fit in with other musicians - one of the few keyboard tutors for students wishing to get into a band.

for *Sax*

ISBN 1-901690-14-8

A Step By Step Guide To Everything You Need To Know About Being A Sax Player, by David 'Baps' Baptiste. This tutor book packs a punch of information to get you started in sax playing. Great photos and explanations and - great fun!

All our books and videos are available from any good musical instrument retail outlet and can be ordered from any bookshop by quoting the ISBN (see vertical text next to each book image above). If you still have any difficulty obtaining our products either contact our distributors:

Music Exchange Limited
Claverton Road
Wythenshawe
Manchester
M32 9ZA

Or you can write direct to us at the address on the title page - or:

for *Everyone*

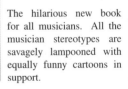

ISBN 1-901690-50-4

The hilarious new book for all musicians. All the musician stereotypes are savagely lampooned with equally funny cartoons in support.

Visit our website - *the* place to start for any music related topic
www.psst.co.uk